SOVIET MILITARY POWER 1990

D1339036

CONTENTS

First Edition	September 1981
Second Edition	March 1983
Third Edition	April 1984
Fourth Edition	April 1985
Fifth Edition	March 1986
Sixth Edition	March 1987
Seventh Edition	April 1988
Eighth Edition	September 1989
Ninth Edition	September 1990

Credited photographs are copyrighted and are used with permission. Reproduction and distribution, in whole or in part, without the express permission of the copyright owner is prohibited.

PREFACE

The ninth edition of *Soviet Military Power* is published at a time of unprecedented economic and political turmoil in the Soviet Union. With that turmoil has come an unusual degree of uncertainty about the future course of the Kremlin's enormous military structure. Any authoritative report on Moscow's military forces and the threat they pose requires a greater degree of sophistication and willingness to deal with nuance than ever before. Neither those who are determined to believe that the Soviets no longer threaten Western interests, nor those who regard the Soviet threat as largely unchanged, will find much support in *Soviet Military Power 1990.*

The ambiguity of the threat encompasses far more than the Soviet Union. As the chance of global conflict recedes, dangers in the developing world are increasing. Challenges to our national security are becoming more diffuse and complex. Instability in the Middle East and elsewhere, terrorism, narcotics trafficking, and weapons proliferation are among the threats that must be taken into account as we reshape defense policy.

At the same time, prudence demands that we focus on the most dangerous challenge to our national security. The military might of the Soviet Union is enormous and remains targeted on the United States and our allies. All evidence indicates that this fact will not change. Furthermore, the threat is no longer clear cut; the implications of change within the Soviet Union are not completely known.

As assessment of Soviet power becomes more difficult, the need for this publication increases. There is first the most obvious requirement to set down in one accessible document all we can appropriately reveal about current Soviet forces, their numbers, deployments, and level of technological sophistication. The use of this information is hardly confined to the United States, or even the West. Recently, as part of a heated exchange with a prominent military figure, Georgi Arbatov used the 1989 edition of *Soviet Military Power* to argue that his own nation's arms production had been excessive. The Soviets once denounced this publication. Now they find it a useful reference.

Second is the need to give interested readers a fuller appreciation of modifications of Soviet military doctrine and capabilities. In some cases, change is profound. For example, with the collapse of Soviet control in Eastern Europe, and the unwillingness of the Kremlin to follow past practices and maintain its power through the use of force, the Warsaw Pact has begun to disintegrate. As a result, threat of a surprise attack against the North

**SOVIET
MILITARY
POWER
1990**

Atlantic Treaty Organization (NATO) has been greatly reduced. Defending his government's actions in allowing Eastern Europe to go its own way, Soviet Foreign Minister Eduard Shevardnadze said, "A bloc that has to be forcibly prevented from disintegrating was not and cannot be a reliable prop in serious matters." This document details exactly what has and has not changed with respect to the Soviet posture toward Europe and considers the character of the Soviet threat to NATO.

In other cases, however, Soviet military power still presents a threatening face. This is nowhere more obvious than in strategic nuclear forces and strategic defense capability. The Soviets continue to modernize strategic forces that support a doctrine designed to threaten our strategic forces. The rhetoric of President Mikhail Gorbachev's reforms and the reality of his military force deployment are in great contrast with respect to strategic forces. This is not surprising. If its military capability were not supported by the largest nuclear arsenal in the world, the Soviet Union would cease to be a superpower. Although Mr. Gorbachev speaks of restructuring, he surely cannot intend to reform his nation into second-class power status.

The Soviet threat is changing, but it is not going away. As we watch that change, dispassionate analysis becomes more, not less, important. *Soviet Military Power 1990*, therefore, includes discussions on the range of factors affecting Soviet forces.

After a brief introduction, the document considers Soviet foreign policy and raises important questions about how the Kremlin now defines its national interest. Next, the document looks at changes in Soviet security policy with emphasis on how that policy has altered the threat in Europe. This is followed by a chapter devoted to the economic foundations of Soviet military power. The USSR's economic crisis will continue to have a major impact on its security policy, so the economic dimensions of Soviet military power are given greater weight in this edition than ever before.

The next two chapters examine the Kremlin's nuclear, strategic defense, and space programs, and its general purpose forces. These chapters also consider the US-Soviet balance in each of these areas. The final chapter offers some general comments on the nature of the threat and discusses prospects for the future.

Since last year's issue, we have gained additional insight into the character of the Soviet military. "Military *glasnost*" has not gone far enough, but there is a greater willingness on the part of the political and military leadership to air problems and disagreements in public. This may be credited to the atmosphere of reform, or to the fact that the difficulties are so great that they simply cannot be kept secret.

For example, domestic support for military service is being called into question. Largely as a result of the Baltic secession movements, antimilitary and antidraft campaigns, and the overt resistance of some local governments (such as Armenia) to the draft, Soviet draft evasion has mushroomed. In his speech to the party congress in July 1990, Defense Minister Dmitriy Yazov admitted that the military's spring draft call up had fallen short, with several thousand no-shows. In Armenia, the turnout was negligible.

In addition, there is clearly considerable disagreement within the Soviet military on a host of fundamental issues, such as the disintegration of Soviet influence in Eastern Europe, the pace of reform in military structure, and *glasnost* itself. Many junior and mid-level officers would do away with the draft altogether and would bar the military from internal police operations. Elements of the Soviet High Command openly oppose many of President Gorbachev's reform efforts. As this document points out, much that was once certain about the Soviet military is now open to debate. It is not clear how that debate will be resolved.

Another area in which we continue to gain insight is the burden of defense on the Soviet economy. The Intelligence Community has estimated that Soviet defense spending has increased steadily over the past 25 years, amounting to 15-17 percent of estimated gross national product (GNP) in the 1980s. In contrast, the official Soviet position has been that the defense spending — and hence the burden — is much smaller. Even the "revised" defense budget released by Gorbachev in 1989 (which quadrupled the previous official number) would mean that defense spending would amount to only 9 percent of GNP. More recently, the Soviets have hinted that the burden is really higher. President Gorbachev himself has admitted to spending amounts equivalent to between 13 and 15 percent of the country's GNP on defense, while some Soviet economists have speculated that the burden may be considerably higher, perhaps as much as 25 percent of the Soviet GNP.

These are awesome figures for a government which cannot even provide enough soap for coal miners. By contrast, during a period of unparalleled economic expansion in the United States, defense was allocated between 5 and 6 percent of our GNP.

There are some indications that this astonishing level of Soviet spending is being reduced. Early in 1989, President Gorbachev announced defense spending reductions of 14.2 percent by 1991. We estimate that Soviet military spending fell 4 to 5 percent in real terms in 1989. Even with these reductions, Soviet defense spending is higher than when Mr. Gorbachev came to power. Most important, spending remains at a level that will permit considerable Soviet force modernization.

That modernization is particularly noteworthy in Moscow's nuclear arsenal and strategic defense capability. The Soviet intercontinental ballistic missile (ICBM) force is undergoing a complete upgrade. This includes the continued deployment of the SS-24, a multiple warhead missile deployed in both a fixed and mobile version, the mobile SS-25, and the new version of the SS-18, which carries 10 warheads. With the enhanced survivability of mobile systems, coupled with greater yield and accuracy of the new model SS-18, the Soviets will retain a credible first strike capability against US silo-based ICBMs and non-alert forces, even if the Strategic Arms Reduction Talks (START) Treaty is signed.

Modernization of the Kremlin's bomber force includes new Bear H and Blackjack aircraft equipped with longer-range cruise missiles. We will probably see some reduction in the total number of bombers in the Soviet force as it removes obsolete bombers and concentrates on qualitative improvements such as its cruise missile force.

This is also the case with the Soviet ballistic missile submarine force. The deployment of the Delta IV and Typhoon, which carry 16 and 20 nuclear missiles respectively, is consistent with the overall trend toward quality over quantity.

The Soviet investment in strategic defenses is about equal to that of its investment in offensive nuclear programs. The Soviets have upgraded their antiballistic missile protection of Moscow into a dual-layered system, the only such system in the world. Moscow also maintains an antisatellite capability, which includes systems that are now able to destroy satellites in low earth orbit.

Research on more advanced systems, such as lasers, underlines strong Soviet interest in the military uses of space. Given what must be very intense competition for defense rubles, Soviet spending in the strategic defense area is indeed impressive and indicates an extremely robust commitment to developing a fully capable missile defense system.

No thorough analysis of the Soviet military can render a simple picture of the current threat. Debates over the future of the Communist Party, the structure of the economy, and the military are commonplace. In such an atmosphere, it is difficult to predict what will happen next month, let alone next year. But as far as Soviet military power is concerned, there are some basic steps that the Kremlin could take that, even in the midst of this uncertainty, would help convince the West of the sincerity of its desire to reduce the threat.

For example, the United States would like to see a Soviet Union that places less reliance on the military. This would mean a military that commands only a reasonable share of the nation's wealth. In addition, the Kremlin should cease its massive military aid programs, which last year totaled roughly $15 billion, to regimes such as Afghanistan, North Korea, Libya, Angola, Vietnam, Syria, and especially Cuba, which is only 90 miles from America's shores. This would go a long way in convincing us that the Kremlin is serious about "new thinking" and tackling its domestic economic problems rather than continuing its traditional geopolitical maneuvers of the Cold War.

Any serious analysis of the Soviet military reveals a picture of vigorous internal debates and uncertain intentions, as well as change and instability. What it does not reveal, no matter how much we might wish it, is an eviscerated Soviet force structure and evaporating threat. The truth is more complex than that. There is certainly reason to be optimistic about the future trend in the Soviet threat. But the facts lead only to the conclusion that the Soviet Union remains an enormous military superpower. The intentions of that regime are changing. But intentions are not enough to support dramatic changes in our own level of preparedness. We must see fundamental and enduring changes in both the capabilities and character of Soviet military power.

Dick Cheney
Secretary of Defense
September 1990

Context of Change

ANDRE DURAND/AFP

The legacy of the Soviet political past collided with *glasnost* and present-day *perestroika* reforms in the expression of this retired Soviet military officer who took the occasion of the 1990 Moscow May Day parade to accuse the Communist Party of being the "people's torturer."

INTRODUCTION

Since *Soviet Military Power* was published last year, much has changed in the Soviet Union and in the world. The images of emerging freedom — East and West Berliners tearing down the Berlin Wall, the Solidarity election victory in Poland, the downfall of Ceausescu in Romania, the departure from Czechoslovakia and Hungary of east-bound trains loaded with Soviet forces, Germany moving toward unification, free elections in Nicaragua — have captured the attention of the world.

The extraordinary events of 1989-90 have profoundly altered the security situation between East and West. The nature and complexity of the alterations can be better understood when framed in the context of key questions. What is happening to Soviet military power? How are changes in Soviet military power affecting Western security interests? What are the implications for the balance between East and West? The answers to these and other questions will shape the new security order in Europe, and frame the debate surrounding such critical issues as the continuing role of the North Atlantic Treaty Organization (NATO), the emergence of a united Germany, and the status of the Warsaw Pact. Outside Europe, similar changes in Soviet military power are less evident but ultimately can be expected to affect regional balances as well. Although a consensus on such questions may be difficult, if not impossible, to reach in the midst of the current turbulence and complexity, it is essential to address them in order to reach any understanding of the changes and the prospects for the future.

SOVIET MILITARY POWER 1990

This year's edition of *Soviet Military Power*, like its predecessors, seeks to describe and assess the current status of Soviet military capability and to derive the implications for the US/USSR military balance. Additionally, this edition reflects the profound, even revolutionary, changes which are occurring in the Soviet Union and Eastern Europe and in their relations with the rest of the world. The essence of these changes is highly elusive because they are so complex, extraordinary, and unprecedented. During the past year the world has witnessed the intense internal struggles of a Soviet Union in crisis, the celebrations of peoples in Eastern Europe starting on the new path to freedom and democracy, and steps by the free world to adjust its security structure within an environment of both new hope and continuing uncertainty.

As a result, Soviet military power must be addressed within a very broad context. Soviet military capabilities are formidable and include the only nuclear arsenal that could destroy the United States and its allies. With the events of the past year, however, attention has been increasingly drawn to the economic and political underpinnings of Soviet military power. Soviet leaders have acknowledged the dismal failure of the communist system to compete with the free market economies of the West. Critical issues of Soviet national security

now focus on stability and restructuring the economy, international cooperation and participation, German unification and new security structures in Europe, trade and economic interaction with the West, and the political as well as military issues involved in force reductions and arms control. This edition of *Soviet Military Power* addresses these fundamental and compelling issues driving Soviet security policy and military capabilities.

The presentation and analyses of the issues in the following chapters generally focus on five fundamental questions:

- What has and has not changed?
- What do these changes mean?
- What trends and directions can be identified?
- How do these developments affect the military balance between the US and USSR?
- What are the prospects for the future?

In Chapter II, Soviet foreign policy is discussed. Changes in the world, especially in Eastern Europe, are dramatic. Former allies in the Warsaw Pact have become more independent of the Soviet Union, transforming the Soviet political and military posture in Europe and elsewhere.

In Chapter III, the basic issues of security policy, strategy, and doctrine are presented to provide a foundation for understanding the fundamental forces for change at work. Changes in Soviet security policy and doctrine have called for a new analytical framework for assessing the transition of Soviet security policy.

Chapter IV explores the underlying strengths and weaknesses of the foundation of Soviet military power through an analysis of Soviet resources and how they are allocated. Extreme economic difficulties have affected the size, capabilities, and disposition of Soviet forces. Understanding the fundamental economic forces for change is key to gauging Soviet priorities on defense spending and evaluating likely directions in future Soviet force developments.

Chapter V focuses on Soviet nuclear, strategic defense, and space programs. Since these programs — which are among the most troublesome to the security

NOVOSTI/SOVFOTO

TASS/SOVFOTO

Protests against Moscow's control over non-Russian republics have multiplied; a demonstration in Baku, Azerbaijan, where ethnic rivalries and nationalistic sentiments have fueled outbreaks of violence, and a rally celebrating the 71st anniversary of Ukrainian unification (inset) illustrate the depth of popular disenchantment with the current political structure. These sentiments have fomented calls for increased sovereignty in several republics.

NOVOSTI/SOVFOTO

This M1986 variant of the T-72 M1 Soviet main battle tank is one of three versions being produced to replace older tanks that are being eliminated. Modern main battle tanks now constitute approximately half of the total Soviet tank inventory and 70 percent of the inventory in the Atlantic-to-the-Urals zone.

of the United States — represent absolute priorities to Soviet leaders, they have been largely exempt from radical changes mandated elsewhere.

In Chapter VI, Soviet general purpose forces are closely analyzed. Some of the developments are very promising, while others are discouraging or reflect little or no positive change. Stated Soviet intentions include reductions in the military budget and military production, projected and actual force withdrawals from Eastern Europe and around the world, reductions in force levels, overall reductions in the threat to NATO, and a willingness to pursue meaningful and verifiable arms control agreements, especially Strategic Arms Reduction Talks (START), initial discussions on a Chemical Weapons Convention, and Conventional Armed Forces in Europe (CFE). These positive elements in the US-Soviet relationship stand in contrast to other developments that cause concern. The Soviets continue to produce high levels of modern military equipment,

NOVOSTI/SOVFOTO

NOVOSTI/SOVFOTO

Lithuanians ask about their status under Gorbachev in 1990 upon the President's arrival in the capital of Vilnius. Baltic separatism poses a compelling challenge to the current structure of the Soviet Union.

The withdrawal of selected Soviet armored forces from Czechoslovakia began soon after the two countries signed a bilateral agreement in February 1990 stipulating that all Soviet troops would be withdrawn by mid-1991.

outnumbering total NATO production in many cases. Developments that have been initially encouraging in force reductions are complicated by Soviet stockpiling east of the Urals, limited destruction of equipment to date, retention in Eastern Europe of elements of disbanded divisions, and operational and political issues associated with the withdrawal of forces from the German Democratic Republic. Furthermore, the ongoing Soviet internal debate over military doctrine, restructuring, training, and modernization is not resolved.

Finally, in Chapter VII, the prospects for the future are discussed. In spite of the uncertainties, it is clear that the Soviet Union still possesses a vast and dangerous military arsenal which must be respected for its capability and its potential to greatly damage US interests. How fundamental and enduring the changes in Soviet military capabilities will be is the critical question.

While hopes are high, we must remain mindful of the continuing security problems posed by Soviet military power.

II

Soviet Foreign Policy

NOVOSTI/SOVFOTO

The Soviet Union's architect of change, Mikhail Gorbachev, was sworn in as President March 15, 1990. Gorbachev has used his new office to demonstrate much greater flexibility and initiative in Soviet foreign policy, introducing a new perspective on the effort to promote Soviet security goals.

OVERVIEW

The debate over the most effective means to ensure Soviet national security is central to the ongoing reform process within the Soviet Union. Soviet leaders have reevaluated the importance of their military power in achieving national objectives. They understand that maintaining expensive, large, offensively postured con-

ventional military forces in Europe hinders their ability to meet their economic and political objectives. As a result, the Soviet leadership shows evidence of relying more heavily on achieving Soviet security objectives through what some officials have termed "negotiating down the threat" that Moscow perceives, rather than on maintaining large, expensive, and offensively postured conventional and strategic forces. This chapter examines the transition in Soviet foreign policy — what has changed and what has not changed.

The foreign policies by which Moscow has pursued Soviet security interests have varied substantially over the course of Soviet history. During the Brezhnev era, in the belief that the international "correlation of forces" had shifted in their favor, the Soviet leadership coupled a massive and sustained arms buildup with assertive and adventuresome international policies. In an effort to make the USSR the dominant political power in Europe, for example, the Soviets maintained and significantly improved enormous conventional forces opposite NATO in Eastern Europe and the USSR, intervened militarily in Czechoslovakia in 1968 and maintained forces there in the ensuing years, and supported a decade of severe repression in Poland. Moscow also deployed SS-20 intermediate-range mobile nuclear missiles that altered the European military balance, and at the same time waged a propaganda campaign of political warfare against NATO counterdeployments. Similarly, in an effort to exploit targets of opportunity and advance communism in key locations, the USSR shipped large amounts of military hardware to Third World client states, pledged support to "national liberation movements" that frequently resorted to terrorism, entered into security commitments with Marxist-Leninist regimes in Cuba, Vietnam, Angola, Mozambique, and Ethiopia, and in 1979 invaded Afghanistan.

President Gorbachev has reassessed this interventionist approach. Under his leadership, Soviet foreign policy has demonstrated much greater flexibility and initiative, introducing a new perspective on the effort to promote Soviet security goals and redefining some of the goals themselves. As part of their concept of "new political thinking," the Soviets are seeking to identify areas of mutual interest with the West. ("New political thinking" is a concept that includes the principles of "balance of interests," "mutual security," and "freedom of choice," as well as a rejection of "zero-sum" thinking.) There also has been important progress in Soviet foreign policy in other areas, such as the Soviet withdrawal from Afghanistan, cooperation in the Angola/Namibia settlement, and evidence of repudiation of the doctrines of class warfare and international struggle. The Soviets have also specifically renounced what has been known

in the West as the Brezhnev Doctrine, a policy of intervening militarily in any country where a communist regime was about to be overthrown.

These are important changes; nonetheless, it remains to be seen to what extent Soviet long-range political goals have changed and are compatible with those of the US and the West. In arms control, difficult issues remain, including questions of Soviet compliance. Economic relations with the West continue to be hampered by the slowness of progress in real, market-oriented reform. Extensive illegal activity is still directed toward the acquisition of sensitive Western technology. Soviet intelligence services, including the military intelligence services, are particularly active today in most Western countries.

These apparent contradictions in Soviet foreign policy reflect the extensive debate taking place within the Soviet Union today over the proper nature and mission of the Soviet state. In the past several years, the Communist Party's ideological guidelines for foreign policy have been increasingly discarded. However, a consensus in favor of an alternative has yet to emerge, and the Party remains in control. In this uncertain environment, advocates of a number of differing world views have been competing for predominance in Soviet foreign policymaking. Many Soviet international experts, particularly within the Ministry of Foreign Affairs and the semiofficial Soviet foreign policy institutes, are thought to favor the renunciation of doctrines and strategies that posit a permanent state of conflict with the West, but others, particularly within the Soviet military, intelligence services, and Communist Party apparatus, are thought to continue to favor policies which see the world primarily in ideological terms. It is not yet clear which point of view will ultimately prevail. The basic premise of "new thinking" has been accepted, although the full meaning and implementation of this approach is still being debated, resulting in some inconsistencies between stated intentions and actions.

The changes in Soviet foreign policy have been prompted largely by the internal and external crises facing the Soviet Union. The Soviet leadership faces both an economy in crisis and a nascent, untested political system. Moscow seeks a sympathetic interna-

NOVOSTI/SOVFOTO

Tension showed on the faces of Lithuanian intellectuals whose hopes for independence were frustrated during President Gorbachev's visit to the Baltic republic in January 1990.

NOVOSTI/SOVFOTO

President Gorbachev issued a stern warning to Lithuanian leaders considering a declaration of independence from the Soviet Union, which was followed by an economic blockade of the republic.

tional environment to allow for internal political and economic reform. The USSR desires improved relations with the United States and Western Europe in order to alter fundamentally the nature of relations with the US and the West away from confrontation toward greater cooperation. Also, to improve its domestic economy, the USSR seeks to achieve greater access to international trade, technology, and financial markets and to encourage NATO countries and others to reduce their defense expenditures.

Soviet foreign relations are influenced as well by Moscow's policies toward the many nationalities and religious groups residing in the Soviet Union. The Soviet crackdown in Azerbaijan in January 1990 and Moscow's policies in Soviet Central Asia have affected adversely Moscow's relations with the Islamic world. Moscow's past repression of Soviet Jews had a negative effect on Soviet relations with Israel and the West for many years, while the Soviet Government's new liberalized emigration policy has affected adversely Soviet relations with the Arab world. The Soviet economic blockade and political intimidation tactics used in the Baltic states in the spring of 1990 hampered Soviet efforts to draw closer to Western Europe.

The United States has welcomed the important steps which have been taken in the Soviet Union toward democratization, economic reform, military reductions, and changing foreign policy approaches. President Bush has made clear that as the USSR moves toward democracy and openness, US policy envisions going "beyond containment" and looks forward to welcoming the Soviet Union into the broader "commonwealth of nations." The United States remains hopeful that Gorbachev's program of *perestroika* will lead to genuine po-

litical pluralism, openness, and a free market economy.

SOVIET FOREIGN POLICY IN PRACTICE

Within the framework of the "new political thinking," several concepts have been articulated which represent significant breaks with the hardline rhetoric that has traditionally justified or defined Soviet behavior. The Soviets now assert, for example, that all countries should be free to choose their own policies. Soviet spokesmen also now cite the importance of developing good relations with all states, regardless of their ideological affiliation, and of seeking to play a constructive role in regional and other issues. In practice, "new political thinking" has produced greater Soviet diplomatic flexibility, fostering more constructive approaches to many international issues.

In the area of foreign military assistance, although support currently continues at a high level, the Soviets have begun cutting back. For example, the value of Soviet military aid to Third World countries dropped to $15 billion in 1989, about $2 billion below the previous year's figure. Lower shipments to Iraq and other Middle East states accounted for the drop. Andrei Grachev, Deputy Chief of the International Department of the Communist Party Central Committee, said in May 1990 that Moscow is putting less emphasis on its relations with the Third World in light of political changes in Eastern Europe and the Soviet Union. He indicated that foreign military assistance programs would be subject to a very radical review in the near future. Nevertheless, it is not yet completely clear how much the Soviet cutback in foreign military aid is due to the economic troubles the Soviets face at home as opposed to a real change in long-term goals.

Furthermore, it is unclear to what degree cuts in foreign military assistance grants could be translated into gains for the Soviet economy. Thus, the cost-benefit analysis for granting military aid often involves political issues as much as fiscal ones. Moscow probably will continue to provide grant military assistance if there can be a net political gain.

US-Soviet Relations

President Gorbachev's program of "new thinking" includes as one of its goals improved relations with the United States. The US has welcomed the new Soviet openness. US-Soviet relations in 1990 have expanded considerably, and the US and USSR now have the most extensive set of contacts and discussions since the end of the Second World War. Washington and Moscow now hold regular discussions on a wide range of issues and have made progress in a number of areas of mutual interest. Although arms control talks are probably the best known element of this relationship, other US-Soviet discussions focus on regional issues, human rights issues, and bilateral and transnational issues as well.

Progress in this Soviet-American relationship continued during Soviet Foreign Minister Eduard Shevardnadze's visit with Secretary of State James Baker in Wyoming in September 1989, during the meeting between President Bush and President Gorbachev off the coast of Malta two months later, in Ministerial-level meetings in early 1990, and at the May 30-June 3 Bush-Gorbachev Summit in Washington. In Wyoming, the United States proposed that the US and the USSR both adopt a policy of "Open Lands," by which the United States and the Soviet Union would reciprocally eliminate most restrictions on travel by officials of the other side. At Malta, President Bush sought progress toward improved relations in the areas of economic and commercial relations, human rights, regional issues, arms control, and the environment. At the Washington Summit, numerous agreements were reached including:

- A pledge to slash stockpiles of chemical weapons;
- A statement on the main elements of the forthcoming strategic arms control agreement;
- A statement of objectives for follow-on strategic arms talks that commits both countries to pursue stabilizing reductions in the number of multiple nuclear warheads on strategic missiles;
- A statement pledging to accelerate work to enable completion of a Conventional Armed Forces in Europe (CFE) agreement by 1990;
- A pledge to work together against proliferation of

nuclear, chemical, and ballistic missile technologies; and
- A commercial accord that, upon taking effect, will facilitate trade between the two countries.

United States support has been provided to the Soviet effort to institute democratization, economic reform, and legal reform, and improve the Soviet human rights record. Senior Administration officials have visited the USSR to make American experience in these areas available to the Soviets. Progress has also been made over the past two years toward greater US-Soviet cooperation in curbing proliferation of missile technology, chemical weapons, and nuclear weapons, and in addressing global environmental problems.

The growing US-Soviet dialogue provides a useful forum for encouraging Moscow to continue reducing the Soviet military threat and to play a more constructive role in international affairs. The United States has been urging the USSR to take a number of specific steps toward this end that include:

- Developing a force posture which is reduced in size, less threatening abroad, and more reflective of reformist intentions at home;
- Releasing more information on Soviet military reforms and budgets; and
- Refraining from the threat or use of force against the territorial integrity or political independence of any state.

The United States has developed a multilevel dialogue with the Soviet defense establishment and a program of military-to-military exchanges for the purpose of promoting several important goals:

- To encourage the Soviet Union to develop defensive doctrines, strategies, and operational planning;
- To urge the Soviet defense establishment to take steps toward "military *glasnost*" — openness in defense budgets, planning, strategy, and operations;
- To impress upon the Soviets that US security objectives — the protection of the US and its allies, and advancing freedom and democracy — are benign; (This includes making known the true defensive nature of United States military doctrine, demonstrating the defensive structure of US forces, and displaying the capabilities of US weapon systems to help increase Soviet understanding of United States defense policy.)
- To impress upon the Soviets the openness of US defense planning, including the public disclosure of the defense budget and the open congressional review which follows;
- To make known to the Soviets the limited role of the

A US Air Force F-15 escort guides a Soviet MiG-29 Fulcrum fighter through North American airspace en route to a US air show.

military in a free, democratic society; and
- To promote better understanding through human contacts between military officials of the two countries at all levels.

In support of these policy goals, an unprecedented program of military-to-military contacts was instituted between the US and Soviet armed forces and defense ministries. In June 1989, for example, then-Chairman of the Joint Chiefs of Staff Admiral William Crowe visited the Soviet Union, where he signed the US-Soviet Agreement on the Prevention of Dangerous Military Activities. In October 1989, Secretary of Defense Dick Cheney welcomed General of the Army Dmitriy Yazov in the first official visit ever by a Soviet Minister of Defense to the United States. There have been numerous other meetings and exchanges at various levels, and also exchanges of port visits by US and Soviet warships.

Arms Control

Significant progress has been made in various negotiations, particularly the Strategic Arms Reduction Talks (START). The provisions already agreed to in START include central limits on nuclear delivery vehicles (1,600) and warheads (6,000); and sublimits on heavy intercontinental ballistic missiles (ICBMs) (154), ICBM and submarine-launched ballistic missile (SLBM) warheads (4,900), and mobile ICBM warheads (1,100). The aggregate throwweight of deployed ICBMs and SLBMs will also be cut to 50 percent of the current Soviet level.

The progress thus far in the START negotiations

demonstrates that the United States is within reach of achieving its goals of enhancing strategic stability and strengthening peace and international security. A START Treaty, for which President Bush and President Gorbachev have pledged to complete negotiations by the end of 1990, will characterize a relationship between the United States and Soviet Union that is more cooperative, predictable, and stable.

The United States remains concerned about the Soviet Backfire bomber, SS-18 modernization, and agreement provisions that could affect US alliance relationships. The manner in which the Soviets resolve these outstanding issues will be an important indicator of their ability to deal constructively in the arms control arena, and to implement the Treaty once completed.

Even as arms control negotiations with the USSR progress, however, it is important to consider the matter of Soviet compliance with previous arms control obligations. For example, the Soviet Foreign Minister has admitted that the Krasnoyarsk radar is an illegally situated radar in clear violation of the Antiballistic

With their tail sections severed, obsolete M-4 Bison long-range bombers no longer count as part of the Soviet Union's manned strategic bomber force.

TASS SOVFOTO

Missile (ABM) Treaty of 1972. The Soviet Government has also stated that SS-23s, a weapon system covered by the Intermediate-Range Nuclear Forces (INF) Treaty of 1987, were located in Eastern Europe prior to the signing of the Treaty. The Soviet violation at Krasnoyarsk, Soviet violation of the Biological Weapons Convention (BWC), and Soviet failure to advise US negotiators about the transfer of these INF missiles call into question Soviet good faith in negotiating arms control agreements. The Soviets have indicated a willingness to address some of these concerns by initiating destruction of the radar and by making an effort to resolve our concerns about violation of the BWC.

In the Defense and Space Talks (DST), the US seeks to facilitate a cooperative transition to a more stabilizing balance of strategic offensive and strategic defensive forces. Although serious differences remain, the Joint Statement on Follow-on Strategic Negotiations released at the Washington Summit reflected Soviet agreement to continue the DST "without delay," with the objective of "implement(ing) an appropriate relationship between strategic offenses and defenses."

NOVOSTI/SOVFOTO

Destruction of Soviet intermediate-range and shorter-range missiles (the destruction of an SS-20 is shown here) has continued with implementation of the INF Treaty.

In chemical weapon (CW) negotiations, the US and the Soviet Union made significant progress at the Washington Summit in 1990. President Bush and President Gorbachev signed an agreement that calls for the destruction of most US and Soviet chemical weapons by 2002. Destruction will begin by the end of 1992, and at least 50 percent of the stocks must be destroyed by the end of 1999. Neither country will be permitted to produce chemical weapons once the agreement takes effect. Currently, the Soviets possess the most extensive chemical warfare capability in the world and have acknowledged an aggregation of at least 40,000 tons of chemical munitions.

Important progress has been made toward a CFE agreement. The Soviet Union and the other members of the Warsaw Pact have agreed to seek the establishment of a secure and stable balance of forces at lower levels, the elimination of disparities prejudicial to stability and security, and the elimination, as a high priority, of the capability for launching a surprise attack and for initiating large-scale offensive action.

The 23 participants in the CFE negotiations agreed that the categories of equipment to be limited under the CFE Treaty will include main battle tanks, armored combat vehicles, artillery, combat aircraft, and attack helicopters. There is agreement on the concept of regional sublimits on equipment concentrations, and on the need to establish limits on equipment stationed in Europe. Furthermore, the West and the East have both proposed limits on the equipment held by individual participants — limits that will affect only the Soviet Union, since no other country in Europe even approaches its levels of equipment holdings. Both sides also agreed on the need for an on-site inspection regime to monitor treaty limits.

Many details relating to these provisions remain to be worked out, but significant progress on the basic content of a CFE Treaty has been made. The Soviets have publicly stated that they place a high priority on the CFE negotiations, and have agreed to try to meet the goal of signing a treaty this year.

Europe

For most of the post-war period, Soviet policy toward Europe was dominated by Marxist class-based views supported in Eastern Europe by the Red Army, the KGB, and Soviet-imposed communist regimes. Whereas NATO has always been a voluntary association of democratic states enjoying common political goals, the Warsaw Pact from its inception in 1955 has been little more than a vehicle for Soviet military domination of Eastern Europe. Gorbachev's decision in 1989 to renounce the Brezhnev Doctrine reflected a fundamental change in the Soviet approach.

As a result, the likelihood of East-West military conflict along the European Central Front was reduced significantly in 1989 and 1990. The removal of obstacles to a united Germany in NATO, progress toward West European economic integration, and the increasing dissolution of the Warsaw Pact have reduced tensions in Europe and offer opportunities for a new relationship between Europe and the USSR. At the same time, the extensive political changes taking place within the Soviet Union and Eastern Europe involve significant uncertainties.

Eastern Europe changed dramatically over the past year. Steady political pressure in Poland and Hungary, and popular uprisings in East Germany and Czechoslovakia, resulted in the first free elections in these countries in over 40 years. Democratically elected governments were in place in all four by mid-1990, with the communist parties retaining only small representation. In

NOVOSTI/SOVFOTO

Intensive East-West negotiations over the past year, beginning with talks between Soviet Foreign Minister Eduard Shevardnadze (center), with interpreter (right), and his West German counterpart, Foreign Minister Hans Dietrich Genscher, led to West German Chancellor Helmut Kohl's Moscow meeting in July when the Soviets agreed that a unified Germany may continue as a member of the NATO Alliance.

SOVIET ARMS CONTROL OBJECTIVES

Political

- **Enhance the image of the USSR as a reliable participant.**
- **Employ arms control fora to demonstrate the "new thinking" in foreign and domestic policies.**
- **Remove the US nuclear umbrella from Western Europe.**

Military

- **Eliminate or curtail key US strategic forces and programs including the Strategic Defense Initiative.**
- **Enhance military capabilities but at lower force levels.**
- **Negotiate asymmetric US general purpose naval force reductions.**
- **Eliminate US theater and tactical nuclear systems from Europe.**
- **Impede US and NATO force modernization plans.**
- **Prevent NATO from deploying advanced-technology weapons.**

Economic

- **Enable allocation of some resources from the defense to the civilian sector.**
- **Improve opportunities for access to Western technology and capital.**
- **Establish a more predictable environment in which to plan force modernization and expenditures.**

Bulgaria and Romania, the freest elections in 40 years led to coalition governments, but ones dominated by successors to the Communist Party.

In 1989, Soviet and East European regimes began taking preliminary steps to reduce the enormous conventional forces which had been built up to solidify communist rule and intimidate Western Europe, and the movement toward popularly elected governments accelerated the process. Although Gorbachev pledged in December 1988 to reduce Soviet forces in Eastern Europe by 50,000 men, for example, the Czechoslovak and Hungarian Governments in early 1990 pressed Moscow to withdraw all Soviet forces; the Soviets agreed to timetables that call for Soviet forces to leave Czechoslovakia and Hungary by the end of 1991. In addition, Poland, East Germany, Czechoslovakia, Hungary, and Bulgaria announced in 1989 that they would cut their force levels significantly — ranging from a cut of 9,000 in Hungary to one of 40,000 in Poland — with more cuts expected.

Although some East European political and military leaders believe that the Warsaw Pact may be useful during the transition to a European security structure, an increasing number recommend its rapid abolition, and the Pact no longer represents an integrated, reliable military command. The Warsaw Pact's military structure has not disappeared, but cooperation and contact between Soviet military officials and officials of East European members of the Pact appear to be diminishing. The Soviets are no longer assured of the reliability of the non-Soviet Warsaw Pact allies to support Soviet political and military goals. Moscow could not count on any East European military to participate in, or even tacitly support, an attack against NATO countries.

Soviet relations with Western Europe have improved markedly over the past several years. Moscow's decision, as part of the December 1987 INF Treaty, to destroy all of its intermediate- and shorter-range missiles and launchers, and the Soviet withdrawal from Afghanistan in February 1989, addressed two obstacles to improved Soviet-West European relations which had existed for a decade. Moreover, Moscow's acknowledgement in July 1990 that a united Germany should have the right to be a member of NATO marked a watershed in Soviet relations with the West. Gorbachev's stated commitment to use peaceful means to resolve problems of foreign policy has improved the perception of the USSR in Western Europe. Moscow's expectation of favorable Western responses to improved Soviet conduct has provided an incentive for restraint in Soviet policy.

One of the most important examples of East-West contact was the Military Doctrine Seminar, conducted under the auspices of the 35 participating Conference on Security and Cooperation in Europe (CSCE) states in the Confidence- and Security-Building Measures (CSBM) negotiations. This landmark seminar was an unprecedented three-week session (January 16-February 5, 1990) during which the Chairman of the Joint Chiefs of Staff, General Colin Powell, met with his NATO and Warsaw Pact counterparts, and others, to discuss conventional doctrine and force posture.

Moscow is promoting the integration of the USSR into the European economic and political system as well as the development of a new Pan-European security framework. The Soviets seek to build new mechanisms and institutions through the CSCE process to help the USSR maintain influence in European affairs. Although the Soviets recognize that reliance on the 35-state CSCE will dilute the role of both superpowers in Europe, they view CSCE as a forum that would guarantee them the opportunity to press their own economic and security interests and initiatives. Attempts to aggravate European relations with the United States are exemplified by Soviet pressure on naval arms control and advocacy of nuclear-free zones in Europe.

Regional Policies

Soviet regional policy reveals elements of both continuity and change. Until the ascendance of Gorbachev,

Soviet regional policy was strongly influenced by a desire to expand Soviet influence and access, and characterized by extensive arms transfers and support for indigenous Marxist-Leninist parties or radical national liberation movements and client states. During the Brezhnev era, the Soviets attempted to expand their influence in the Third World through direct application of military force or by supporting client and East Bloc forces. The Soviet invasion of Afghanistan, the transport of Cuban forces to Angola and Ethiopia, backing for the Vietnamese invasion of Cambodia, and support for the Sandinista regime in Nicaragua's subversion of its neighbors in Central America are perhaps the most notable examples. Moreover, there was a steady rise in military assistance programs of all types, including Soviet aid to the communist regime in Cuba.

Today, Soviet policy toward the Third World is in a state of transition. In 1989, the USSR withdrew its military forces on schedule from Afghanistan, assisted in the agreement to remove Cuban forces from Angola, and supported the withdrawal of Vietnamese forces from Cambodia. In addition, the Soviets have reduced their level of military forces in Cam Ranh Bay, Vietnam. In spite of increased aid to some client states, including Afghanistan, Cambodia, and Ethiopia, the Soviets reduced their total level of military assistance in 1989.

The USSR now appears to believe that it needs to court potentially important states regardless of their ideology or the sentiments of traditional friends. The primary Soviet objective in regional affairs appears to be to strengthen and broaden links with emerging powers, and to identify potential areas of cooperation with the United States. At the same time, Moscow is likely to continue striving to increase its power and influence at the expense of the West — through diplomacy, economic and military aid, and limited support of movements hostile to Western interests.

Soviet behavior is driven both by the primacy of domestic economic reconstruction, which requires a more benign and stable external environment and reduced foreign aid expenditures, and by the desire to preserve a claim to superpower status and a key role in all regional affairs. As a result, the Soviets have increasingly turned to the United Nations and other multilateral fora, particularly in cases where Moscow was overcommitted to clients bogged down in civil wars with little chance of securing victory. Nevertheless, Soviet policy in Afghanistan suggests that the USSR may still be prepared to make available large quantities of military equipment to clients in regional conflicts under certain conditions.

Debate in the USSR concerning the expense of Soviet Third World policies began during the Brezhnev era but has taken on operational significance only recently. The Soviets will probably continue to be a major arms exporter during the next few years, although it is likely that they will provide less grant military aid — now totaling over $8 billion per year — in favor of greater reliance on cash sales. Soviet clients have been seeking more sophisticated and costly systems, and Moscow seems prepared to comply, particularly for those who can afford some form of cash repayment. Moreover, Moscow appears reluctant to relinquish the potential influence or hard-currency earnings that its military exports provide.

Moscow's continued willingness to provide large amounts of economic assistance to certain selected states seems more doubtful. To date Soviet net economic assistance to key clients like Cuba, Vietnam, North Korea, and Cambodia, has not wavered: Moscow provided on average the equivalent of over $10 billion annually during 1985-89 (though much of this was in fulfillment of prior obligations). The Soviets are trying to shift the emphasis in economic aid programs away from grant assistance to poorer radical clients and toward joint venture programs with more economically successful Third World countries. They are also strengthening their ability to obtain sensitive military technologies from countries capable of developing them. In any case, Soviet policy changes toward the Third World are those most easily subject to change.

The changes in Eastern Europe have eliminated an important avenue for Soviet support to radical clients. The new East European Governments have begun cutting political, economic, and military support to Soviet clients who cannot pay with hard currency or commodities. Should this trend continue, the cost of Soviet efforts to provide current levels of political, military, and economic support for some clients will increase. Moreover, Moscow will not be able to count on East European diplomats, intelligence personnel, or financial resources to assist Soviet initiatives to the extent that it has in the past.

One area of Soviet regional policy which continues to be disturbing is the continued support for "active measures." The Soviet Union persists in channeling covert support to leftist parties and anti-Western groups in developing countries. Since Gorbachev assumed power, for example, the Soviets have actually increased "active measures" campaigns designed to advance the new Soviet foreign policy goals and undermine Third World support for United States military presence in the various regions.

East Asia and the Pacific

Moscow is seeking to expand its role in East Asia and the Pacific in an effort to gain assistance in Soviet economic development and to increase Soviet influence in the region. Since the historic May 1989 Sino-Soviet Summit in Beijing, Moscow has remained committed to further improving relations with China, despite differences over the pace of political reform in the Soviet Union. Other Soviet efforts in the region have been slowed by Moscow's reluctance to make significant concessions on contentious issues such as the return of the Northern Territories to Japan and the scope and form of foreign economic participation in development of the Soviet Far East. The offensive potential of Soviet sea and air forces located adjacent to Japan and Korea also continues to pose an obstacle to better Soviet relations with states in the area.

Soviet policy appears to be shifting toward a new strategy that emphasizes improving relations with non-communist countries, especially Japan and South Korea, and enhancing security in the Far East. Soviet officials stress their interest in establishing a regional arms control mechanism, increasing cooperation with the Association of Southeast Asian Nations (ASEAN), participating in multilateral economic organizations, and resolving the Cambodian conflict. In addition, as part of the 500,000-man unilateral reductions that Gorbachev announced in December 1988, Soviet forces east of the Urals are to be cut by 40 percent by January 1991. While the force reductions in this region have thus far progressed rather slowly, they appear to be proceeding generally in accordance with Gorbachev's stated commitment.

Middle East and South Asia

Under Gorbachev, Soviet policy in the Middle East and South Asia seeks to promote Soviet objectives without alienating the United States. The Soviet withdrawal from Afghanistan; increased overtures toward Egypt, Israel, and Saudi Arabia; a joint call with the US for peace in Lebanon; Soviet cooperation with the United States and other nations in opposing Iraqi aggression; and some reduction in Soviet support for states such as Syria and Libya, represent important changes from earlier Soviet practices.

For the most part, Moscow has not actively obstructed United States efforts to promote an Arab-Israeli settlement. However, the Soviet sale of advanced Su-24 light bombers to Libya in 1989, Soviet arms sales to Iraq through much of 1990 in spite of the Iraqi development and use of chemical weapons, and the continuing Soviet military relationship with Syria complicate efforts to reach a settlement.

In South Asia, Soviet policy has long given preference to India, whose links to the Soviets remain strong. In the wake of its withdrawal from Afghanistan, the USSR is now also seeking to improve damaged relations with Pakistan and other Islamic states in the region, although continued Soviet support for the Najibullah regime in Afghanistan remains a major obstacle to the normalization of relations with these governments.

Africa

During the Brezhnev era, Moscow's involvement in sub-Saharan Africa focused heavily on military assistance for Marxist-Leninist allies — Angola, Ethiopia, and Mozambique. Though declining, military aid still dominates Soviet policy toward the region.

The USSR is trying to maintain its influence in Angola and Ethiopia while prodding these states to negotiate an end to their respective civil wars. The Soviet Union continues to provide military assistance to the Marxist regime in Angola (hundreds of millions of dollars), and military advisers contributed to Angolan military operations against the anticommunist National Union for Total Independence of Angola (UNITA) insurgency in the December 1989 offensive. While pushing the Popular Movement for the Liberation of Angola (MPLA) toward direct talks with UNITA, Moscow has made clear its unwillingness to support a military solution to the war.

Ethiopia was the largest sub-Saharan recipient of Soviet military assistance in 1989, receiving well over half a billion dollars. Moscow has concluded, however, that the war is unwinnable and that Ethiopia should seek a political solution. Military advisers are being withdrawn, but Soviet air crews still provide limited logistical support, and Moscow retains the naval facility at Dahlak Island.

In South Africa, the Soviets have cultivated improved relations with Pretoria while also maintaining their relationship with the African National Congress. Significantly, Moscow no longer advocates an armed struggle and is positioning itself to influence the transition to a post-apartheid government. As elsewhere in Africa, Moscow is trying to keep its options open.

Latin America

Soviet leaders believe conditions favor the expansion of their influence in Latin America through enhanced state-to-state ties, economic cooperation, and efforts to reduce tensions with the United States. At the same time, Moscow faces constraints on its ability to adopt new policies.

Soviet economic assistance to Cuba — approximately $5 billion per year — drains Soviet resources by diverting them to the inefficient Cuban economy that supports the Castro regime. Castro has resisted calls for economic or political reform, choosing instead to continue his course of confrontation with the United States.

Despite problems in the political and economic spheres, Soviet-Cuban strategic and military ties remain firm. Moscow views Cuba as a long-term investment of great strategic value and has been reluctant to reduce its military presence or intelligence-gathering apparatus. The Soviets continue to help improve Cuba's air, antiair, and naval capabilities. Soviet shipments of MiG-29 advanced fighter aircraft to Cuba in 1989 increased the threat to the region and indicated the limits of "new thinking." Soviet indications that aid to Cuba will be reduced are a positive sign and may enhance US-Soviet cooperation on economic and other issues.

In Central America, after several years of promoting tensions, the Soviet role has become less obstructionist. In 1989 and 1990, Moscow encouraged the Sandinista Government in Nicaragua to hold free elections. The Soviets probably did so in the expectation of a Sandinista victory, but following the election of a democratic government, they have offered continued economic aid. However, a decline from previous Soviet assistance levels of almost $1 billion per year is expected.

PROSPECTS

Soviet foreign policy has reflected the uneven progress evident throughout the Soviet reform process. There has been a clear desire to improve relations with the United States and Europe. The Soviets have also taken concrete steps to enhance their image as a less threatening global participant. As a result, the likelihood of a conflict stemming from US-Soviet confrontation is lower than it has ever been in the post-war era. On the other hand, there is ample evidence that "new thinking" has not changed every aspect of Soviet foreign policy. It appears the Soviets now seek a calmer international climate in order to address the economic and political concerns plaguing them internally and externally. However, there remain contradictory trends in Soviet policy and continuing temptations to advance Soviet interests at the expense of the West.

Soviet Security Policy in Transition

GAMMA LIAISON

As democratic reforms sweep through former communist regimes in the countries of Eastern Europe, and the Warsaw Pact collapses as a viable military alliance, Soviet military forces have begun withdrawal from some forward bases. Here, equipment of a Soviet division is loaded aboard trains prior to departure from Czechoslovakia.

INTRODUCTION

Soviet policy and doctrine underlie all decisions relating to force structure and use of military power. Much has changed over the last decade in the way the Soviet leadership views itself and the world, and this has been reflected through fundamental changes in policy and doctrine. This chapter reviews these changes and their rationale largely through what the Soviets themselves are saying and through the limited evidence available. Although somewhat speculative, since evidence does not yet indicate whether or not the prospective changes will actually occur and endure, an understanding of this conceptual framework is essential in order to identify trends and to interpret adjustments in Soviet force structure.

The chapter provides an overview of Soviet security policy in transition and examines the incentives for change, the military policy transition itself, and the direction of that transition. It concludes with a discussion of current issues and concerns and prospects for the future.

OVERVIEW

In promising a less threatening force posture, the Soviets have stated that they have adopted a defense doctrine that reflects a concept of "reasonable sufficiency." Evidence of this change is reflected in several areas:

- Reduction in the overall size of conventional forces and reductions scheduled to be completed by the end of 1990;
- Decreased overall spending and military production, as well as the limited conversion of some military production facilities to consumer goods;
- Withdrawal of Soviet forces from Afghanistan;
- Agreement to withdraw all Soviet forces from Hungary by June and Czechoslovakia by July 1991;
- Agreement to withdraw Soviet forces from the present territory of the German Democratic Republic within three to four years; and
- Reduction of forces in Mongolia and various parts of the USSR.

On the other hand, the Soviet concept of a defensive doctrine seems to apply only to conventional forces, not to strategic forces. The Soviets have not announced reductions in strategic forces, as they have in conventional forces; indeed, they are continuing to maintain and modernize their arsenal of strategic nuclear weapons and have refused to agree to the elimination of first-strike-capable heavy intercontinental ballistic missiles (ICBMs). With respect to conventional forces, the Soviet military started at a much higher level, relative to forces of other countries, of over 5,000,000 military personnel, 211 divisions, and the highest levels of tanks and certain other equipment in the world. Even with their announced unilateral reductions, the level of their forces will still outnumber those of any other country in the world, and indeed the entire NATO Alliance, in many categories of forces.

Thus, there are many ambiguities and uncertainties about the current and future course of Soviet military forces, programs, budgets, and production. There is much that we in the West do not know about current Soviet military programs and even more that we do not know about what will happen to Soviet military forces in the five-year plan for 1991-1995. President Bush and others have proposed that the USSR apply *glasnost* to the Soviet military and publicly release information on the Soviet military similar to what the US Government releases on the US military. Release of such information could improve mutual understanding and help demonstrate the true nature and direction of Soviet military programs.

SOVIET SECURITY POLICY AND INCENTIVES FOR CHANGE

Shortly before the 1988 Reagan-Gorbachev summit meeting in Moscow, Georgi Arbatov, the Director of the Institute for the Study of the USA and Canada, told American reporters that "we are going to do something terrible to you. We are going to deprive you of an enemy." This is indicative of what appears to be a major revision in Soviet military doctrine, initiated by the political leadership. Although there are serious legitimate concerns in the West about these changes, the situation holds great promise for reducing international tensions and the arms buildup that resulted from over 40 years of aggressive Soviet foreign and military policies.

The realization that the Soviet approach to national security triggered a counterproductive military response from the West has led the Soviets to adopt a policy that is a striking departure from the traditional Soviet fixation on "antagonistic contradictions" in determining military sufficiency. President Gorbachev's redefinition of national security in the nuclear age constitutes a direct challenge to the "zero-sum" assumptions that shaped the traditional Soviet military approach to security. This was explained by a lead editorial in a General Staff journal:

Security in the nuclear age must be evaluated differently. Assessing security is more and more becoming a political task. It can only be resolved

TIMELINE OF KEY EVENTS

February 1986
Gorbachev announces that Soviet military force developments would be based on the principle of "reasonable sufficiency."

May 1987
The Soviets announce a new "defensive" military doctrine.

June 1987
The Soviets announce that future military force developments would emphasize quality over quantity.

May 1988
The Soviets start to withdraw forces from Afghanistan.

December 1988
Gorbachev delivers UN speech announcing unilateral withdrawals and reductions of Soviet forces.

January 1989
The Soviets announce cuts in their overall military budget and military production (baseline for the cuts not given) through 1991.

February 1989
The Soviets complete troop withdrawals from Afghanistan.

May 1989
The Soviets make first CFE proposal that includes deep cuts in Soviet/Warsaw Pact forces.

The Soviets announce a 77.3 billion ruble defense budget for 1989.

June 1989
The Soviets start to withdraw from Mongolia.

The Soviets announce for the first time the breakdown of their defense budget (O&M, R&D, personnel, procurement, etc. for 1989)

August 1989
Poland appoints a noncommunist prime minister.

September 1989
The Soviets announce a 71 billion ruble defense budget for 1990.

October 1989
Hungary abandons the leading role of the Communist Party.

November 1989
The Berlin Wall comes down.

The Czechoslovak Communist Party Presidium and Secretariat resign en masse.

Long-time Bulgarian leader Todor Zhivkov is removed from his party and government posts.

December 1989
Old line communist leaders in East Germany resign.

US President and Soviet President meet off the coast of Malta.

A noncommunist (Vaclav Havel) becomes President of Czechoslovakia.

The Ceausescu Government in Romania is overthrown by force.

January 1990
The Polish Communist Party dissolves itself.

February 1990
The Bulgarian Communist Party Chairman and senior leadership resign.

The Soviet Union and Czechoslovakia sign a bilateral agreement for the withdrawal of all Soviet troops by mid-1991.

March 1990
The Soviet constitution is amended deleting the reference to the leading role of the Soviet Communist Party.

The Soviet Union and Hungary sign a bilateral agreement for the withdrawal of all Soviet troops by mid-1991.

East Germany holds free elections.

Hungary holds free elections.

April 1990
Poland holds free local elections.

May 1990
Romania holds purportedly free elections.

Talks between East and West German leaders and Four Powers begin.

Yeltsin is elected Chairman of Supreme Soviet of the Russian Republic.

May 30–June 3, 1990
US-USSR Washington Summit.

June 1990
Romanian protesters are violently suppressed.

Bulgarian Socialist Party (former Communist Party) wins elections.

July 1990
German Economic and Monetary Union is implemented.

The Soviets drop their objections to full membership by a united Germany in NATO.

August 1990
Moscow supports UN economic sanctions against Iraq and imposes arms embargo.

by political means through detente, disarmament, strengthening confidence, and developing international cooperation.

This recognition not only heightens the importance of political as distinct from military-technical variables in the security calculus, but places unusual emphasis on threat reduction, unilateral restraint, and collaboration with adversaries. Not since the "nuclear revolution in military affairs" has there been such an intense national debate in the Soviet Union over the direction of force development.

Between the 1960s and the mid-1980s, Soviet wartime objectives included the defense of the territory of the Soviet state and that of its allies and the achievement of military victory in the event of war. Military victory required the achievement of several strategic objectives to include the total destruction of the enemy's armed forces, occupation of key regions of his territory, and

imposition of post-war peacetime conditions. Implicit in this concept of victory was the survival of the Soviet state and political system, which, in the view of Soviet military and political leaders, would be problematic at best if the war were to escalate to massive use of nuclear weapons.

Soviet military thinking envisioned the outbreak of a conventional war near the Soviet periphery, which would subsequently escalate to nuclear use on a theater scale, followed quickly by a massive global nuclear exchange. Given these expectations and the need to reconcile the requirements to achieve victory in war and preserve the Soviet state, Soviet military strategy has been directed toward attaining victory with conventional arms under the constant threat of the enemy's use of nuclear weapons. The Soviet concept of operations focused on rapid destruction of much of NATO's nuclear capabilities concurrent with a deeply penetrating conventional ground offensive. The Soviets were very

Soviet Operational Concepts
Traditional Offensive Strategy and New Declared Defensive Doctrine

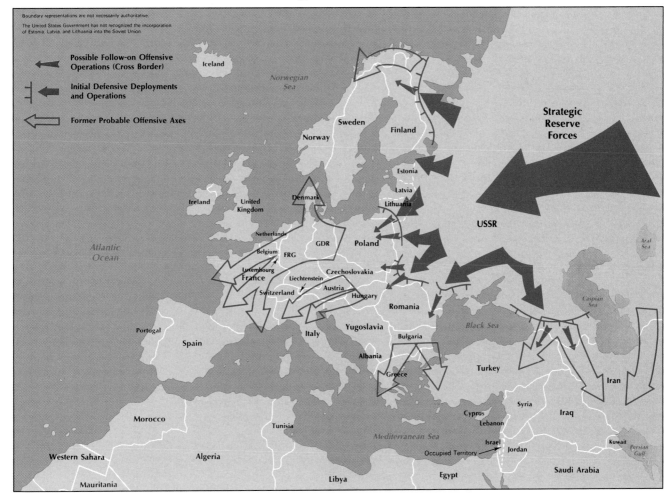

strongly disinclined to initiate nuclear use as long as the enemy maintained a survivable nuclear retaliatory capability. Soviet planners were extremely pessimistic about the ability of combatants to avoid escalation after initial nuclear use by either side.

Changes in Soviet military doctrine and strategy began to evolve well before Gorbachev became General Secretary, and Soviet statements of their doctrine now stress war prevention and defense far more than did the doctrine of the 1970s and early 1980s. Soviet military strategy still includes the concept of the counteroffensive to repel enemy aggression, but the traditional concept of victory appears to be in the process of redefinition. The definition of victory in Soviet doctrine may eventually encompass less ambitious objectives that include the successful defense of Soviet territory, including the possibility of counteroffensive operations that may cross state boundaries, accompanied by early war termination before either side has escalated to nuclear use.

The reasons for this change spring from two key areas of concern to the Soviet leadership: military-technical and political-economic. The military-technical concerns appear to have grown out of strategic appraisals made in the early- to mid-1980s by the political leadership as well as the military. Since the Soviets firmly believed that nuclear escalation would effectively deny achievement of the wartime strategic objectives, it apparently was deemed necessary to question traditional military assumptions and expectations about the ability to control escalation on the battlefield. The concept that a Warsaw Pact strategic conventional offensive could pre-emptively deny NATO any incentive to initiate nuclear use was viewed to be questionable at best.

Until the mid-1980s, the dominant, although possibly contested, Soviet military approach toward achieving a capability to fulfill its doctrine involved attempts to add and restructure forces. The Soviets also developed operations, such as deep penetration by operational maneuver groups (OMGs) designed to seize key objectives that included airfields and other nuclear-related facilities and control centers before NATO's nuclear weapons could be used. Soviet deployment of tactical nuclear artillery within the Warsaw Pact beginning in 1982 may also have been expected to help restrain NATO's early use of its own nuclear artillery. At the same time, while the Soviets sought to reduce the size of the US strategic nuclear arsenal through negotiations to help reduce the scale of destruction of the USSR should escalation control fail, the Soviets continued their unprecedented buildup in strategic nuclear forces.

This wartime strategy of a pre-emptive conventional

strategic offensive, largely associated with Marshal Nikolay Ogarkov (Chief of the General Staff between 1977 and 1984), led to the NATO perception that the magnitude and immediacy of the Warsaw Pact threat had increased considerably. As a result, NATO responded politically and militarily. Politically, NATO demonstrated increasing coherence and resolve most clearly in the deployment of Pershing II and ground-launched cruise missiles (GLCMs) in 1983. Militarily, the US and NATO took deliberate steps to increase the capabilities and readiness of their conventional and nuclear forces. Soviet military behavior helped to spur US investment in high-technology conventional weapons and nuclear modernization.

As a result, Soviet military planners anticipated the decreasing likelihood of a rapid conventional victory in the event of war, raising the prospect of a conventional stalemate and possible wartime dissolution of the Warsaw Pact alliance. At the same time, they could expect increased danger of nuclear use, given NATO's greatly increased nuclear readiness. In the area of global strategic forces, the Soviet military's confrontational posture in Europe severely undermined support in the West for major reductions in intercontinental strategic nuclear systems. More disturbing, perhaps, the force-building approach had probably increased the likelihood that war would occur.

In addition to the military-technical, the second and more widely acknowledged major source of change of Soviet military doctrine and strategy was the political-economic. The economic costs of building and sustaining the military forces required to support a confrontational "victory"-oriented strategy had become increasingly burdensome. In addition to the direct costs of the military's seemingly insatiable demands on scarce material and human resources were the indirect economic costs imposed by relative political and economic isolation from the prosperous, technologically advanced economies of the West.

The relative significance of the military investment burden becomes clearer in light of recent Soviet acknowledgements of the extremely poor and now declining performance of the Soviet economy over the past three decades. The Soviets have not only been suffering from the well-documented liabilities of a command economy, but according to some Soviet economists, as much as 25 percent of their gross national product (GNP) may be directed to the military sector. Gorbachev and his supporters understood that the military burden had contributed significantly to the stagnation and decline of the Soviet economy and living standards while directly and indirectly undermining the overall defense posture of the Soviet state. In addition, poor economic performance and isolation from the technologically advanced West had led to the serious erosion of the technology base and, consequently, had severely undermined long-term Soviet competitiveness in advanced military applications of new technologies.

To overcome these effects, since 1985 the Soviet political leadership has sought to define defense and strategy more broadly in terms of political, economic, and social considerations. This new definition of a more comprehensive view of national security complemented Gorbachev's "new thinking" in foreign policy which advocated transition to a less confrontational, more defensive posture around the Soviet periphery to reduce both the risk of war and the potential for nuclear escalation.

There has been general consensus on the need to change military doctrine and strategy. The friction that has been evident between key members of the military and political leadership under President Gorbachev over these changes has basically evolved from differences over professional prerogatives, issues of East-West reciprocity, the military's contention that NATO remains a serious military threat, and the pace and magnitude of change. It has not been over the nature and direction of the change itself. Implementation of the new doctrine will continue to be the source of bureaucratic conflict within the new, broader national security establishment of the Soviet Government.

SOVIET MILITARY POLICY IN TRANSITION

President Gorbachev's policy of *perestroika,* or restructuring Soviet society, has been applied to the area of military doctrine, strategy, and military development as it has to all other spheres of Soviet society. Some Soviet political leaders have advocated bringing military policy more in line with economic and international political realities. Many Soviet civilian reformers have criticized previous Soviet policies for excessively emphasizing military preparation for a future war, while down-playing the role of political means for achieving national security objectives.

The deployment of SS-20 missiles and the invasion of Afghanistan are cited by Soviet civilian critics as examples of an excessive tendency in Soviet foreign policy to rely on military force. At the political level, the policy flowing from this "new thinking" reflects the thesis that the Soviet Union has no valid reason to remain in a state of class confrontation with the US or any other country. At the military level, the central question is how the political objectives of preventing war

The Congress of People's Deputies, shown here, is a forum for open discussion of political issues. The Supreme Soviet, no longer a rubber stamp for programs of the Soviet leadership, is also becoming a forum for debate and action as its delegates address the Soviet Union's new political and foreign policy directions under *perestroika.*

and strengthening strategic stability can be reflected in the development of strategic and operational concepts for the armed forces and plans for mobilization of industry.

Institutionalizing the Search for Alternative Means of Security Decisionmaking

By broadening the Soviet perspective on national security, President Gorbachev has reduced the ability of the professional military to pre-emptively shape the discussion of national security policy. While noting that "reform will take time, education, and patience," Foreign Minister Shevardnadze has declared that "we are no longer going to let our military do all the job. There will be no more monopoly."

One of the two key aspects of the strategy to change national security decisionmaking has been to encourage the emergence of institute specialists as influential experts on security issues. Evidence of this is the elevation of two former directors of the Institute of World Economy and International Relations to the Presidential Council and increasing the number of institute specialists on the Central Committee, Supreme Soviet, and in the Ministry of Foreign Affairs (MFA).

The second new mechanism for defense decisionmaking came into being in June 1989 with the establishment of the Defense and State Security Committee (DSSC) of the new Supreme Soviet, and has already become

TASS/SOVFOTO

Debate over the future orientation of the Soviet military and "defensive sufficiency" has extended beyond the military to include prominent civilians such as Georgi Arbatov.

a factor of some consequence in the struggle to establish civilian oversight of military policy. A July 1988 "scientific-practical" conference of some 1,000 top officials of the military, intelligence community, the MFA, and institute specialists paved the way for the DSSC and put the campaign against the General Staff monopoly on threat definition into high gear. In a speech to the conference, Foreign Minister Shevardnadze argued that:

> There is a need to introduce a legislative procedure in accordance with which all departments engaged in military and military-industrial activity would be under the control of the highest nationwide elective bodies. This applies to use of armed force outside the country's borders, defense development plans, and openness of military budgets where they are linked mainly with the problem of national security.

The Committee has a full agenda and still lacks the expertise and authority to exercise full civilian control.

THE NEW MILITARY DOCTRINE

Military doctrine in the Soviet Union provides political guidance to the armed forces on the likely character of a future war, potential opponents, force development, and employment concepts. It identifies both general political objectives of a future war as well as the specific military-technical preparations necessary to meet those objectives. Soviet military doctrine is not immutable and has undergone a number of changes over the last 30

years in response to evolving political, economic, and military-technical realities.

Although defense of the USSR and primacy of Party rule have always been pre-eminent political objectives, military-technical considerations have played the dominant role in Soviet force development throughout much of the post-war period. For most of this time, the emphasis has been on the conduct of large-scale offensive operations on enemy territory as the best method to secure wartime Soviet political objectives. Consequently, military doctrine in the Soviet Union has provided the political rationale for the unrelenting development and modernization of both nuclear and conventional weapon systems, the deployment and maintenance of an enormous force structure in both Eastern Europe and on the Sino-Soviet border, continuous growth in Soviet military expenditures, and the development and further refinement of overtly offensive employment concepts. In short, from the beginning of the post-war period, Soviet military doctrine has played a critical role in the development of the very "enemy image," both held and projected, that President Gorbachev has over the last five years gone to such lengths to reduce.

Not surprisingly, a fundamental revision of Soviet military doctrine became an early objective of President Gorbachev's new approach to national security. Two years of discussion in the Soviet Defense Council preceded the announcement of a new military doctrine at a Warsaw Pact meeting in May 1987. At a Foreign Ministry conference reported by the Soviet press in January 1989, however, Foreign Minister Shevardnadze indicated that the doctrine had not yet been fully elaborated even by the time of President Gorbachev's United Nations speech in December 1988. Then at the January 1990 Conference on Security and Cooperation in Europe/Confidence- and Security-Building Measures (CSCE/CSBM) Military Doctrine Seminar in Vienna, Army General M. A. Moiseyev, Chief of the General Staff, claimed the Soviet military now operates under a new set of principles. These sharply contradict previous core premises of Soviet military doctrine, and it remains to be seen if and how they will actually affect Soviet military strategy and deployment. The guidelines were as follows:

- War is no longer considered a means of achieving political objectives.
- The Soviet Union will never initiate military actions against any other state.
- The Soviet Union will never be the first to use nuclear weapons.
- The Soviet Union has no territorial claims against nor

LEGISLATIVE OVERSIGHT OF THE MILITARY IN THE USSR

The Committee on Defense and State Security chaired by Leonid Sharin, is part of a legislative system that is still in its infancy. The Committee was created in June 1989 to help draft legislation involving military and security issues and to oversee the activities of the Ministry of Defense, KGB, and police. Committee membership is dominated by officials from these organizations. Over half of its 43 members are professional military, representatives of defense/heavy industry, or KGB officers. There are three subcommittees: Armed Services (chaired by a civilian — scientist Yevgeniy Velikhov); Defense Industry (headed by defense industry manager Mikhail Simonov); and State Security (headed by regional party chief Grigoriy Kharchenko).

The extent to which the Committee evolves into a real oversight body able to play an aggressive role in the strategic decisionmaking process depends in part on the evolving authority of the Supreme Soviet and developments affecting other players in the defense policy system (the President, the Presidential Council, the Defense Council, and the Party leadership bodies). Also important are the policy preferences of its members, many of whom reflect the relatively conservative, pro-military biases of the military-industrial institutions that employ them. Most deputies involved in the Committee lack the time (many are still carrying out the responsibilities of their original jobs) and experience to provide aggressive oversight. Moreover, those military officers who have taken a critical stance

toward the armed forces have come under considerable pressure from the military. The Committee also has very limited staff and technical support.

Nonetheless, the Committee has probably benefited from the apparent downgrading of the USSR Defense Council, which previously dominated defense decisions. Moreover, as Committee members and staff gain experience, the Committee will be better able to function as an independent check on the military. Additionally, the apparent determination of the more activist Committee members (coupled with pressure from other reform-minded legislators) likely will prod the Committee into assuming a more powerful role in the decisionmaking process.

---

does it consider any other state to be its enemy.

- The Soviet Union seeks to preserve military parity as a decisive factor in averting war, but at much lower levels.

Consequently, according to Soviet strategists, war prevention, in place of war preparation, has emerged as the pre-eminent political objective of the new doctrine. Although this objective is to be achieved primarily through a combination of political and diplomatic measures, the military has not been relieved of its primary mission of defending the USSR in the event that war prevention fails.

This new doctrine forces the military to forego its exclusive emphasis on offensive operations. Instead, the new political guidelines mandate that the Soviet armed forces focus on the conduct of defensive operations to repel aggression during the initial period of any future conflict. The military has not, however, conceptually relinquished the necessity for the preparation of a subsequent strategic counteroffensive, which calls for training and capabilities similar to those which would be needed for an offensive attack. Although the Soviet military continues to assert its control over the military-technical component of doctrine, forces and employment concepts are to be structured in such a way as to prevent escalation, provide an opportunity for the political leadership to negotiate a solution, and terminate a conflict at the lowest possible level of destruction.

The military-technical component of the new doctrine is structured to provide guidance in four basic areas:

- Nature of the threat;
- Character of future war;
- Force development; and
- Methods of armed conflict, training, and preparation.

Today, the imprint of the new military doctrine is most visible in the latter two areas, although the political leadership hopes that its new approach to security will also shape the direction and context of the first two.

Nature of the Threat

Threat definition, as a key starting point for future force planning, remains a subject of debate between civilians and the military establishment within the Soviet Union. The civilian leadership and national security advisers worked to persuade others that "new political thinking" has achieved a reduction of the East-West military confrontation and has had a direct impact on Western military programs. All appear to agree that the direct threat of war, which the Soviets professed to believe was quite high earlier in the decade, has now receded significantly. These civilians point to proposed reductions in the US defense budget and program cuts to support their view that "new political thinking" is having a stabilizing effect on the external threat environment.

THE PRESIDENTIAL COUNCIL AND THE DEFENSE COUNCIL

A series of constitutional amendments adopted on March 14, 1990 created a Soviet president who is also the supreme commander in chief of the armed forces. Under the new system, the president has the power to coordinate the activities of those institutions involved in defense and to declare mobilization, war in the event of an attack on the USSR, martial law, and a state of emergency in a particular region. The president has an advisory body, responsible for elaborating "measures to implement the main directions of the USSR's domestic and foreign policy and ensure the country's security."

The fate of the USSR Defense Council under the new system appears to still be under consideration. Those portions of the Constitution dealing with the Defense Council — article 113, point 3, and article 121, point 5 — were deleted. Several Soviet spokesmen, including Gorbachev himself, implied that the Defense Council has been disestablished by the new provisions and its role taken over (at least in part) by the Presidential Council. The membership of the Presidential Council includes some of those officials previously involved in Defense Council decisionmaking, such as the Chairman of the Council of Ministers, Defense Minister, Foreign Minister, Chairman of the KGB, and Minister of the Interior. However, the mission of the new Presidential Council (which met for the first time on March 27, 1990) is far broader than the Defense Council. This is reflected in its membership, which includes economic advisers and cultural figures. Moreover, missing from the membership of the Presidential Council are Chief of the General Staff Mikhail Moiseyev and other military leaders.

It is possible that the Defense Council is being reconstituted as a defense subcommittee of the Presidential Council. On April 10, 1990, Gorbachev stated that "questions of defense have been devolved to the functions of the President as Commander in Chief, but the working body, the Defense Council, operates under the President." This measure might have been an attempt to placate military leaders who were concerned that the new constitutional arrangement deprived defense issues of a top-level decisionmaking body dedicated solely to security-related affairs.

Senior Soviet military leaders, on the other hand, have continued to insist that, while the threat of immediate war has receded, the military danger to the Soviet Union has not significantly decreased and may, in fact, be growing. In the military's view, this increased military danger is inherent in the exponential improvements in lethality and effectiveness of new weapon systems. Moreover, they believe continued regional instability and conflict are compounded by the increasing weapons technology available to the Third World. In short, the military argues that increasing international uncertainty and instability force them to retain sufficient combat potential to fulfill any and all missions levied on the armed forces by the political leadership.

The outcome of this debate between the civilian and military leadership over the nature of the "threat" to the Soviet Union will critically influence the direction of Soviet security policy. In any case, the determination of the military to preserve its capabilities against its alleged adversaries appears inconsistent with the new cooperative approach to security policy and a reduced emphasis on the use of force.

Character of Future War

While the Soviet political leadership appears to have forced doctrinal changes on the military, the Soviet General Staff's assessments of the character of future war have yet to exhibit any major changes. They continue to assert that the means employed in such a war could be either nuclear or conventional, although widespread nuclear use would produce catastrophic results. Precision-guided munitions and high-accuracy conventional systems are likely to assume a greater role in any future conflict, even supplanting nuclear weapons as the weapons of preference in the execution of certain missions.

The Soviet military leadership believes that a conflict is likely to be protracted and lead eventually to a strategic nuclear exchange. Therefore, the incentives are high for ending a conflict before it escalates to a competition of relative industrial bases for the production of high-technology weapons.

Force Development

The Soviet approach to force development for the past two decades has been based on balanced, but steady growth of each of the services of the armed forces. The objective of this growth has been to support the execution of large-scale offensive operations to defeat enemy armed forces and to occupy enemy territory in the event of a future conflict.

At the 27th Party Congress in 1986, Gorbachev declared that henceforth Soviet force development would be based on the principle of "reasonable sufficiency." Gorbachev and his advisers, however, failed to provide a specific definition beyond the stipulation that the armed forces would no longer have the capability for surprise attack or the conduct of large-scale offensive operations. The provision of more specificity for "reasonable sufficiency" quickly became an issue of major contention between the military and civilian defense analysts.

This issue was resolved to some extent at the 19th Party Conference in 1988. At that time, the political leadership decreed that future force development would move away from a quantitative emphasis in favor of qualitative parameters. After the Party Conference, Soviet Minister of Defense Marshal Yazov justified the shift in emphasis to quality not only on the basis of cost savings, but also by reference to the fact that the military-technical revolution is rendering quantity less decisive on the modern battlefield. Adherence to the principle of "reasonable sufficiency," therefore, in no way restricts the modernization of Soviet weapon systems or military equipment. The continuing development of the Soviet Navy's aircraft carrier program and the continued introduction of modern equipment into the ground forces, air forces, and strategic rocket forces indicate that the military has succeeded in imposing its interpretation of "reasonable sufficiency" on the Soviet force development process.

"Reasonable sufficiency" seems to apply, however, primarily to the quantitative development of Soviet general purpose forces. It clearly has provided the doctrinal justification for both the unilateral withdrawals of Soviet forces from Eastern Europe and the Sino-Soviet border, the restructuring of Soviet forces to a more defensive orientation, and Soviet proposals in the Conventional Armed Forces in Europe (CFE) negotiations.

Of primary importance to the political leadership, however, is the principle that "reasonable sufficiency" must provide a basis for reductions in Soviet military spending and procurement. The US estimates that after a period of steady growth between 1985 and 1989 of about 3 percent per year, Soviet military spending was cut 4-5 percent in real terms in 1989, while weapons procurement outlays dropped 6-7 percent. The Soviets have also announced a series of cuts notably in the procurement of tanks, ammunition, helicopters, and infantry fighting vehicles.

Methods of Armed Conflict, Training, and Preparation

According to the new military doctrine, defensive operations would dominate during the initial period of a future conventional conflict. Prior to the adoption of the new military doctrine, the Soviets viewed defense primarily as a forced type of military action, to

be conducted only temporarily until conditions could be created to return to decisive offensive operations. Since 1987, however, they have asserted that this new "defensive doctrine" has led to revised operational-strategic plans, basic planning documents, and combat regulations. Training, according to Soviet presentations at the January 1990 CSCE/CSBM Military Doctrine Seminar, has also been restructured in line with a new defensive orientation. The Soviets state that the number of large-scale exercises has dropped off significantly — Army-level and below exercises were down substantially in 1989 from a level of 40 operational and tactical exercises in 1986. Also, the number of strategic nuclear forces' missile launches was halved in 1989, and training manuals and documents for use at Soviet military academies have been revised in line with the new orientation. These statements are generally consistent with Western observations.

As with "reasonable sufficiency," however, there are a number of unresolved issues with regard to this component of the new doctrine. First, the Soviets are not renouncing entirely the concept of offensive actions. The military argues, for example, that even large-scale operational counterstrikes are a fundamental component of any defensive operation designed to halt and repel an aggressor. However, according to Soviet presentations at the CSCE/CSBM Military Doctrine Seminar, these offensive actions would take place only within the context of a larger-scale defensive operation.

Second, the military has been unable to resolve the fundamental contradiction between the politically mandated disavowal of surprise attack and the requirements associated with the struggle to seize the initiative in the event of any future conflict. Soviet military art has traditionally viewed surprise attack as the best method for seizing the initiative and dictating the subsequent course of a conflict. The objective has been to stun an opponent initially and then to press the attack in order to prevent that opponent from recovering his balance and regrouping his forces for an effective defense or counterattack. Furthermore, in spite of renunciation of preventive or pre-emptive attacks at the CSCE/CSBM Military Doctrine Seminar, it appears the Soviets intend to seize fire superiority over an enemy from the outset of any conflict, most likely through the conduct of pre-emptive targeting of enemy deep-fire systems. At a minimum, this suggests that the politically mandated disavowal of surprise attack has not yet been completely correlated with traditional Soviet operational requirements.

Third, the Soviets have yet to allay Western suspi-

SOVIET MILITARY REFORM:
TACTICAL ADJUSTMENT VERSUS RADICAL TRANSFORMATION

DEFENSE MINISTRY PROPOSAL	RADICAL VERSION OF MILITARY REFORM
Manning	**Manning**
■ Retains conscription, but conscripts in selected posts would have a choice between serving a 2-year fixed term or a 3-year term under contract. ■ Has vague provisions for alternative service.	■ Creates a smaller military manned by volunteers. ■ Creates territorial units in the ground forces. ■ Creates a territorially based reserve.
Defense decisionmaking	**Defense Decisionmaking**
■ Strengthens power of USSR President.	■ Civilianizes the post of Defense Minister.
Republic Autonomy	**Republic Autonomy**
■ Reaffirms centralized control of military. ■ Rejects possibility of creating national or territorial units.	■ Gives each republic the right to conclude a treaty with Moscow covering defense issues. ■ Subordinates territorial units and reserve forces to both Moscow and the republics.
Personnel	**Personnel**
■ Has harsher penalties for harassing servicemen and their families. ■ Allows officers to leave service voluntarily. ■ Reduces general officers 30 percent.	■ Gives military personnel the right to join trade unions and political parties. ■ Reduces the number of political officers. ■ Eliminates many privileges of the top leadership.

cions that large-scale counteroffensive operations will not be extended into offensive operations into Western Europe. It is evident that the Soviet General Staff has concluded that stationed forces in peacetime are insufficient for the conduct of offensive operations, but are well suited to the achievement of defensive objectives and operations in the initial period, or first few weeks, of war. The General Staff has remained relatively unspecific on the course and conduct of military operations in any subsequent period of war, referring to the possibility of conducting counteroffensive operations, if the political leadership is unable to achieve a negotiated settlement. The West must consider the possibility that the intention of defensive operations during the initial period of war might be to secure sufficient time for the Soviets to mobilize and deploy forward sufficient forces to execute a large-scale counteroffensive.

ISSUES AND CONCERNS

Despite movement toward a more defensive doctrine, the Soviets have continued to develop a strategic nuclear force, as well as command and control structures, that have enhanced survivability — the factor they consider most important in maintaining stability in a crisis or war situation where the imminent employment of nuclear weapons is possible. Extensive and resource-consuming Soviet construction and expansion of deep-underground bunkers for the political and military leadership is continuing. The Soviet deployment of rail- and road-mobile intercontinental ballistic missiles, the continuing construction of nuclear-powered ballistic missile submarines, and the production of modern intercontinental bombers will result in the creation of a highly survivable strategic nuclear force.

Moreover, Soviet military planners have not given any signs of reducing their efforts to achieve a qualitative leap in military capabilities by developing a new generation of weapons based on emerging advanced technology. Likewise, they appear determined to develop a fundamentally new class of weapons by exploiting new, cutting edge technologies such as plasma, directed energy systems, and biotechnology in order to be prepared for what they see as a revolutionary change of the nature of the future battlefield.

Soviet military reformers have yet to address a number of important issues, such as the role of military procurement prices relative to the general price reform in any transition to a market economy. The losses involved in undervalued wholesale prices for military acquisition are generally covered by hidden state loans and they are never repaid. Ending subsidies to defense industries that are paid abnormally low prices for the hardware they produce for the military would allow the assessed value of production to rise to the actual cost of production. This may force a contraction of conventional forces to sustain military research and development funding.

The establishment of an all-volunteer force in the context of significant reductions has also been raised. Reducing ground forces would allow the professionalization of the military while also avoiding the tensions between Soviet republics generated by the large semiannual call up. In turn, a more professional force would permit employment of more sophisticated weaponry and simplify current command and control problems.

The professionalization of Soviet armed forces is an aspect of military reform which has engendered spirited debate. Two competing proposals are being drafted by commissions of the General Staff of the MOD and the Defense and State Security Committee. Under these proposals volunteers will constitute a larger part of the armed forces, the political control apparatus will be reorganized and reduced, and the republics will enjoy greater control over defense issues (for example, home stationing).

The more radical version being drafted by the DSSC Commission is the work of lower-level officers under the outspoken Major Lopatin. It envisages the transfer of the Soviet military to an all-volunteer system within four to five years and would civilianize the post of Defense Minister. The Defense Ministry's proposal is predictably more conservative and foresees a gradual phase-in of changes over the next 9 to 10 years; however, it reflects some concessions to the reformers, incorporating a provision shifting selected conscript posts to billets filled on a contractual basis. The concessions probably reflect the high command's perception that significant change in the military system is inevitable, and a desire to have an input in the reform process and delimit a basis from which to negotiate.

EASTFOTO

As part of the first stage of Soviet troop withdrawals from Hungary, Soviet infantrymen and their personnel carriers were loaded aboard a train in Hajmasker, Hungary in March 1990.

PROSPECTS

Numerous factors have coalesced to compel the Soviets to adopt a security policy that now includes internal as well as external factors. Domestic crises including the economy, nationalism, Party integrity, and the host of issues that emanate from these, are bringing the Soviet Union to the brink of economic breakdown and potential internal chaos. As a result, the Soviets are developing a policy and strategy that is oriented toward defense of the USSR and away from external adventurism. Although still supporting regimes in Angola, Cuba, and Afghanistan, they cannot afford to support the spread of communism externally to the extent they have previously.

As a result of changes in the Soviet Union, the demilitarization of the Warsaw Pact, and the democratization of Eastern Europe, long-held Western objectives have been achieved. But there are too many uncertainties associated with the shift in Soviet security policy and internal unrest for the West to assume that the Soviet Union no longer has the potential to do harm to free world interests. While the Soviets will probably continue along the path of democratization and military reform, albeit inconsistently, they will pursue policies that, from their perspective, enhance their security interests. What is not clear is the ultimate direction their perceptions will lead them.

The Economic Foundations of Soviet Military Power

Under *perestroika,* the Soviet leadership has identified selected military production cuts as part of the restructuring of the Soviet economy. Thus far, few facilities, such as this MiG-29 plant, have been converted for use within civilian industry.

INTRODUCTION

Decades of investment priorities skewed to promoting the rapid buildup of military power in the Soviet Union have created a military giant that now overburdens a civilian economy crumbling from neglect. The accumulated problems which resulted from decades of centralized economic planning plus the burden of achieving military superpower status have combined to threaten the foundations of Soviet military and political power. Indeed, critical economic problems are the underlying catalysts of many of the historic military and political changes that are now occurring in the Soviet Union.

In trying to control all aspects of the economy from Moscow, the huge, overcentralized, self-perpetuating bureaucracy has mismanaged a resource-rich nation toward economic disaster. Misdirected investment policies have hobbled the economy with an aging civilian industrial infrastructure increasingly less capable of competing in the international arena and incapable of meeting the growing needs and demands of a work force disenchanted after decades of sacrifice. Widespread breakdowns in transportation and distribution have long interfered with the delivery of output from producers both to factories and to final consumers. Rational economic decisions by plant managers remain impossible because prices are set arbitrarily and do not reflect real costs. Subsidized prices on energy and raw materials, for example, encourage waste and mask the need for conservation. While effective in the past in directing bountiful and cheap resources to priority programs, the central planning system has proven inept at raising the general level of productivity and incapable of adapting rapidly and efficiently to resource stringencies and changing international political and economic conditions.

This chapter provides an assessment of the economic factors influencing Soviet decisions in the security arena. While Gorbachev's announcements on cutting defense are largely in response to strong economic pressures and represent his intention to redirect resources to economic needs, they also most certainly further Soviet efforts to constrain Western military modernization, give added impetus to the arms control process, and enlist Western support to help salvage the USSR's economy. In light of these political implications, it is essential for the West to consider closely the Soviet military-economic reforms. The potential for significant changes in traditional Soviet military resource allocation priorities must be analyzed carefully to ascertain the factors that will help shape future Soviet military power.

THE SOVIET ECONOMIC CHALLENGE

In the five years since Gorbachev first raised expectations in 1985 with his visions of economic reform, the Soviet Union remains a resource giant mired in an inefficient socioeconomic morass. To date, reform efforts have succeeded only in undermining the discipline of the command economy, while proving insufficient to provide the benefits of a market system. As a result, many traditional economic problems have been made worse. Stagnation and decline now prevail in nearly all sectors of the economy. Petroleum production — an important hard-currency earner — is down, as is housing construction. Despite plans to conserve on resources and consolidate priority investment projects, investment spending continues to be wasted as local authorities disperse resources over an enormous number of new projects while ongoing projects stand unfinished. Although the production of consumer goods and services has increased, Soviet citizens have ample reason to believe living conditions have become much worse because not all these consumer goods being produced are reaching the market and because the far larger increase in money incomes has led to an even greater imbalance between demand and supply in the consumer economy. As a result, inflation is rising, and long lines, chronic shortages, hoarding, and rationing have become commonplace, along with widespread diversion of supplies from state stores to special distribution systems. In terms of food and consumer goods availability, Soviet citizens consider themselves in many respects worse off today than during the late 1970s and early 1980s — a time Gorbachev called the "period of stagnation."

While many of the problems facing the Soviet economy are not new, the impact they have on the economy has been magnified under Gorbachev's confusing and at times contradictory attempts at reform, and some new problems have been created. In addition to intensified supply and transport disruptions, the reform program has led to a growing willingness by various ethnic and labor groups to advance their own agendas. Soviet workers are increasing demands for economic concessions — more and better housing, food, and consumer goods; safer working conditions; and environmental safeguards — at a time when resources also are desperately needed to promote industrial modernization, energy production, and infrastructure development. As strikers discover the influence they hold through work stoppages or slowdowns, the potential for serious strike-originated economic disruptions grows despite efforts to ban strikes in certain critical industries. In a self-perpetuating cycle, the deteriorating economic situation both contributes to and is exacerbated by rising labor and ethnic unrest, a situation that likely will worsen in scope and intensity in the near future.

Dismal economic performance and lack of progress in economic reform to date have prompted the Soviets to reassess and revise economic policies. With superpower status consisting solely of a military capability resting precariously on a deteriorating economic base, the Soviet leadership has begun to shift its resource allocation strategy toward shoring up the economic foundations of national power. This will entail, as the Soviets have announced, cuts in military spending and military-sector involvement in greater civilian production. Improvements in consumer welfare are seen as the key incentives needed to raise worker productivity to a level where the Soviet Union can compete economically in the world in the next century.

SOVIET MILITARY SPENDING

Until recently, the Soviets provided little information on their military expenditures. In May 1989, Gorbachev released a new accounting of Soviet defense expenditures for 1989 — 77.3 billion rubles — that, while almost four times greater than previously claimed levels, is unrealistically low in comparison with the resources required to equip and maintain a force the size of the Soviet military. The new Soviet budget is only about half the size of Western estimates of Soviet military outlays and likely excludes numerous military-related activities. In addition, the budget probably does not reflect subsidies to the prices paid by the Ministry of Defense for weapons, equipment, and research and development (R&D) work. Despite fervent official Soviet claims that the new defense budget accounts for all military-related spending, the Soviet leadership may be acknowledging a higher level of defense spending as reflected in statements by Gorbachev and then-Politburo

GAMMA/FERRY

Empty meat and produce counters offer stark testimony to a civilian economy crumbling from mismanagement and neglect during decades of priority investment in Soviet military power.

ECONOMIC PROBLEMS OLD AND NEW CONFRONT THE SOVIET LEADERSHIP

Lingering Traditional Problems
- Ineffective Price Structure
- Inefficient Central Planning
- Aging Plants and Equipment
- Supply Bottlenecks
- Resource Stringencies
- Rising Energy Costs
- Agricultural Losses
- High Military Spending
- Low Slavic Birth Rate

New Challenges
- Labor Unrest
- Ethnic Disturbances
- Unemployment
- Crime
- Foreign Competition
- Rapidly Rising Incomes
- Inflation
- Environmental Damage
- Growing Budget Deficits

member Yegor Ligachev in May 1990 that the USSR has been spending 18-20 percent of the country's national income [13-15 percent of gross national product (GNP)] on defense.

During his first four years in office, Gorbachev did not alter the broad-based military modernization effort he inherited from his predecessors. Indeed, statements by Chairman of the Council of Ministers Nikolai Ryzhkov in June 1989 and President Gorbachev in May 1990 indicated that the original 1986-90 plan called for defense spending to grow at a rate about twice that of economic output. According to Gorbachev, this in fact occurred in 1981-85, but adjustments to this plan were initiated in 1987 and 1988 as defense spending supposedly was held level. President Gorbachev announced in January 1989 that a 14.2 percent unilateral reduction in military outlays would be completed by 1991. While the US Government has measured reductions in 1989, there is little evidence indicating any slowdown before 1989.

Soviet military expenditures fell 4-5 percent in real terms in 1989, according to Western estimates. Weapon procurement expenditures, which account for about half of total military spending, bore the bulk of the reduction, falling 6-7 percent. The largest reductions were concentrated in general purpose forces, especially in ground forces equipment. Procurement for strategic offensive forces declined by about 3 percent last year, while outlays for strategic defense remained essentially

TASS/SOVFOTO

A T-54T recovery vehicle is used to push hay into concrete silage trenches at a stock-breeding farm near Moscow.

unchanged. However, despite these reductions, the level of military expenditures remains higher than when Gorbachev came to power and continues to allow for significant force modernization.

The Soviets claim a defense budget for 1990 of 71.0 billion rubles that indicates the Soviets plan to continue with stated unilateral defense spending reductions as they measure them. Since there are conflicting statements by Soviet officials about the time period for completing the 14.2 percent reduction and about the size of the 1988 base-year defense budget, it remains unclear whether the 1990 planned reduction completes the announced unilateral reductions. Some Soviet officials had noted that unilateral reductions would extend into 1991. Following these cuts, Soviet intentions for defense spending through the mid-1990s remain uncertain. Chairman of the Council of Ministers Ryzhkov stated in May 1989 that the Soviet Union will strive to reduce defense's share of the national economy by one-third to one-half by 1995.

With the further deterioration in Soviet economic performance thus far under Gorbachev; a substantial improvement in the economy is unlikely during the 13th Five-Year Plan, and real defense spending cuts in the 1991-95 period will be necessary for the Soviets to meet their goal of reducing the defense burden. In contrast, however, early indicators of the 1991-95 economic plan

suggest that in spite of ambitious growth targets for civilian goods production in defense industry as part of conversion efforts, the value of military production also appears slated for growth as more technologically advanced and expensive systems enter production.

MILITARY PRODUCTION

Soviet 1989 output of military materiel generally fell from 1988, mirroring Gorbachev's January 1989 announcement that output would be reduced. The most pronounced cuts occurred in ground forces materiel. Output of strategic systems was generally level while the number of naval surface units produced actually rose. The production of submarines remained the same. Some of the declines reflect longer-term downward trends; output of conventional ground force equipment as well as helicopters and fighter aircraft have declined since Gorbachev took office in March 1985. However, since 1985 the manufacture of cruise missiles has accelerated.

Ground Forces

The deepest cutback occurred in the production of the premier offensive ground forces weapon, the tank; output was halved from 3,400, as the Soviets had announced, to about 1,700 — which is still twice the annual NATO production. Smaller, but significant,

US ESTIMATE OF SOVIET MILITARY EXPENDITURES AND DEFENSE BURDEN

Because official Soviet defense budget claims are neither sufficiently informative nor persuasive, the US Government continues to develop independent estimates of Soviet defense spending. These estimates do not rely on Soviet statistics. A direct costing (building-block) approach is used that requires the identification and enumeration of the physical elements constituting the Soviet Union's defense effort over time and the application of cost factors to them. To best compare the proportion of economic resources committed to the military in any particular year, burden estimates — military spending as a percent of GNP — are calculated using prevailing (current) prices in those years. Soviet defense budgets — 1989: 77.3 billion rubles, 1990: 71.0 billion rubles — are most likely stated in current prices, although this remains uncertain. Roughly half the size of US estimates of Soviet defense spending, Soviet official budgets imply a level of defense burden that, while still large by international comparison, is considerably less than Western estimates.

cuts occurred in artillery and multiple rocket launcher output. The decline in tank production must be viewed in light of force reductions and reorganization: the Soviets eliminated obsolescent tanks as part of their unilateral reductions, and they reorganized their ground forces enabling the sustainment of force modernization at lower levels of tank production. The overall modest increases in output of antiaircraft (AA) artillery, such as the self-propelled 2S6 30-mm AA gun and surface-to-air-missile (SAM) system, apparently result from increased requirements caused by the conversion of tank units to motorized rifle units. As a result of these changes, the equipment complement of remaining forces will be comparatively more modern.

Missile Forces

The Soviets turned out strategic offensive missile systems in 1989 at or about the same levels as in 1988, emphasizing mobile intercontinental ballistic missiles (ICBMs) while maintaining output of silo-based ICBMs. Output now includes the SS-18, SS-24 (at least through this year), and SS-25 ICBMs and the SS-N-20 and SS-N-23 submarine-launched ballistic missiles (SLBMs). As dictated by the Intermediate-Range Nuclear Forces (INF) Treaty, output of the SS-20 ended, but tactical forces are being provided with increased numbers of SS-21 short-range ballistic missiles (SRBMs). Sea-launched cruise missile output was unchanged from 1988.

Air Forces

Declines were noted in the output of bombers, fighters, and fighter-bombers in 1989. The decline in overall bomber output reflects a lower rate of production, as expected, of the Bear H bomber. Output of the Backfire remained essentially constant, and production of the long-range Blackjack continued at a low rate. The number of fighters and fighter-bombers produced is only about half that in 1980; however, because of the large quantities in Soviet inventory, and the enhanced quality and capabilities of the newer aircraft, such as the Fencer, Foxhound, Frogfoot, Fulcrum, and Flanker, overall force capabilities will not be affected by the lower production. The combat effectiveness of these aircraft is being improved by continued output of Airborne Warning and Control System (AWACS) aircraft.

Naval Forces

In 1989, 21 surface warships and submarines were produced, which compares with the average production rate of 18 units in the preceding eight years. We estimate that in 1989 the Soviets started construction of 20 units in these categories, which represents an increase of three units relative to 1988. However, for two decades, the number of naval ships launched annually has been decreasing, as Soviet ships have become larger and more sophisticated with increasingly complex weapons and electronic suites. Production of Delta IV- and Typhoon-

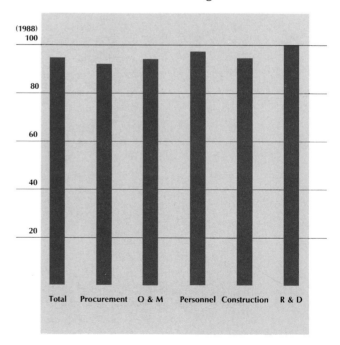

Estimated Soviet Defense Expenditures: 1989 as a Percentage of 1988

class nuclear-powered ballistic missile submarines (SS-BNs) continued strategic submarine force modernization, but the sixth and most recent Typhoon was the last one of that class to be produced. Continued production of Victor III, Sierra, Kilo, and Akula attack submarines, and Oscar II guided-missile submarines has improved antiship and antisubmarine warfare capabilities. Among the surface warships completed was the first Soviet conventional take-off/landing (CTOL) aircraft carrier, the Tbilisi, which will offer improved air defense capabilities. Other completions included another Slava-class cruiser, Udaloy- and Sovremennyy-class destroyers, a Krivak III-class frigate, and Grisha V-class corvettes.

Space

Space launches declined in 1989 from 1988, and the assessed number of space launch vehicles and spacecraft procured in 1989 may have declined as well. However, space launch events are only a partial measure of the Soviet commitment to their space production programs. Many new Soviet satellites produced in the last few years are more capable, reflecting increased sophistication and time on orbit. Hence, the need for replacement spacecraft and the boosters needed to put them into orbit are accordingly reduced. Furthermore, technological problems with new models of spacecraft also affected some recent launch and production activity.

Future Production

Since Gorbachev's announcement in January 1989 of a 19.5 percent cut in production of weapons and military equipment by 1991, there have been a series of Soviet statements on future reductions in output. The overall implications of these statements have been far from clear because they were often contradictory, they seldom noted if the cut was from past output or planned future levels, the time at which the reduction is to occur, and the unit or units of measure for the reduction. At least part of the confusion appears to stem from shortcomings in the Soviet planning process, as well as a continual updating of their reduction program throughout the year. Western assessments of the shape of future Soviet production plans are complicated by the lack of precise and comprehensive data on current production and the imprecision of announced production goals.

In spite of such uncertainties, several general features of the Soviet reduction plan are apparent. First, while the program probably calls for some cutbacks in many types of military materiel, the largest cuts will continue to be in the area of theater force materiel and concentrated in offensive equipment such as tanks. Second, the majority of program cuts probably will take effect during the 13th Five-Year Plan (1991-95). Some evidence from Soviet sources indicates that they may be planning for a moderate increase in at least the value of output during the next five-year plan; such an increase could reflect the entry into production of a new generation of more capable — and hence more expensive — weapons and somewhat increased quantities of defensive equipment such as antiaircraft systems. While it seems that recent Soviet output and their announced plans may mirror a Soviet belief that the Conventional Armed

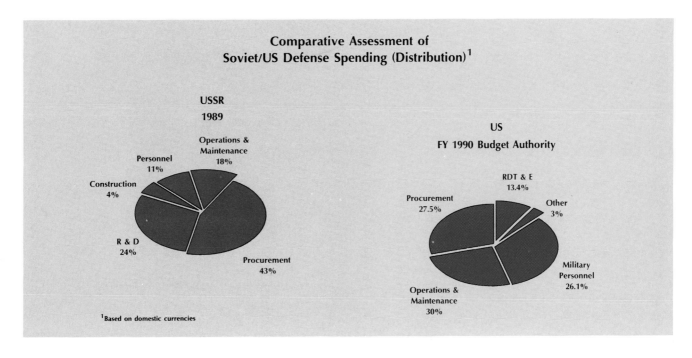

**Comparative Assessment of
Soviet/US Defense Spending (Distribution)[1]**

USSR
1989

Operations &
Maintenance
18%

Personnel
11%

Construction
4%

R & D
24%

Procurement
43%

US
FY 1990 Budget Authority

RDT & E
13.4%

Procurement
27.5%

Other
3%

Military
Personnel
26.1%

Operations &
Maintenance
30%

[1]Based on domestic currencies

Soviet Production 1982–84, 1986–88 and 1989[1]

Equipment Type	Pre-Gorbachev Yearly Average (1982–84)	Gorbachev Yearly Average (1986–88)	Gorbachev (1989)
Tanks	2,800	3,400	1,700
Other Armored Fighting Vehicles	5,400	4,600	5,700
Towed Field Artillery	1,300	1,000	800
Self-Propelled Field Artillery	900	900	750
Multiple Rocket Launchers	600	480	300
Self-Propelled Antiaircraft Artillery	200	100	250
Submarines	9	9	9
Major Surface Warships[5]	9	9	12
Minor Surface Combatants	57	55	54
Bombers	40	47	40
Fighters/Fighter Bombers	950	700[4]	625
ASW Fixed-Wing Aircraft	5	5	5
AWACS	2	5	5
Military Helicopters	580	450	400
ICBMs	116	116	140
SLBMS	115	100	100
SRBMs	580[4]	700[4]	700
Long-Range SLCMs[2]	35[4]	200	200
Short-Range SLCMs[2]	980[4]	1,100[4]	1,100
SAMs[3]	15,000	16,000	14,000

[1] Total military production, including exports
[2] SLCMs divided at 600 kilometers
[3] Excludes man-portable SAMs
[4] Data adjusted to reflect new information
[5] Includes carriers, cruisers, destroyers, frigates, corvettes and paramilitary ships of the same class
As of September 1990

Production of Ground Forces Materiel: USSR and US[1]

Equipment Type	USSR 1987	US 1987	USSR 1988	US 1988	USSR 1989	US 1989
Tanks	3,500	950	3,500	775	1,700	725
Other Armored Fighting Vehicles	4,450	800	5,250	1,000[2]	5,700	650
Towed Field Artillery	900	25[2]	1,100	50[2]	800	60
Self-Propelled Field Artillery	900	225[2]	900	175[2]	750	40
Multiple Rocket Launchers	450	48	500	48	300	47
Self-Propelled Antiaircraft Artillery	100	0	100	0	250	0

[1] Total military production, including exports
[2] Data adjusted to reflect new information
As of September 1990

Missile Production: USSR and US[1]

Equipment Type	USSR 1987	US 1987	USSR 1988	US 1988	USSR 1989	US 1989
ICBMs	125	24[3]	150	12[3]	140	9
SLBMs	100	0[3]	100	0	100	21
SRBMs	750[3]	0	650[3]	0	700	0
Long-Range SLCMs[2]	200	170[3]	200	260[3]	200	420
Short-Range SLCMs[2]	1,100[3]	570[3]	1,100[3]	380[3]	1,100	180

[1] Total military production, including exports
[2] SLCMs divided at 600 kilometers
[3] Data adjusted to reflect new information
As of September 1990

Production of Aircraft: USSR and US[1]

Equipment Type	USSR 1987	US 1987	USSR 1988	US 1988	USSR 1989	US 1989
Bombers	45	52	45	22	40	0
Fighters/Fighter-Bombers	700	550[2]	700	550	625	470
ASW Fixed-Wing Aircraft	5	10	5	5	5	10
AWACS	5	10	5	5[2]	5	2
Military Helicopters	450	360[2]	400	340[2]	400	280

[1] Total military production, including exports
[2] Data adjusted to reflect new information
As of September 1990

Production of Naval Ships: USSR and US[1]

Equipment Type	USSR 1987	US 1987	USSR 1988	US 1988	USSR 1989	US 1989
Ballistic Missile Submarines	2	0	1	1	2	1
GP/Attack Submarines	7	2	7	3	7	5
Other Submarines	0	0	1	0	0	0
Aircraft Carriers	0	0	0	0	1	0
Cruisers	0	4	1	3	1	3
Destroyers	3	0	3	0	3	0
Frigates and Corvettes[2]	5	2	5	0	7	1

[1] Total military production, including exports
[2] Includes paramilitary ships
As of September 1990

A MiG-29 Fulcrum is seen performing a "touch-and-go" landing on the new, 65,000 metric-ton displacement Tbilisi-class aircraft carrier during initial Black Sea flight operations in late 1989.

Forces in Europe (CFE) Treaty will be successfully concluded, force cutbacks well below treaty limits are likely. Such cuts could include armor, artillery, and tactical aircraft units.

THE INDUSTRIAL BASE

Historically, the Soviets have devoted their best resources and most skilled personnel to weapons production. This skewed emphasis has resulted in an increasingly out-of-date manufacturing base for consumer durables and capital equipment. The relative neglect of manufacturing technologies has led not only to a shortage of new machinery needed for civilian production lines, but also to a widening gap with the West in industrial equipment design and production capabilities that threatens the military industrial sector's ability to produce high-technology weapon systems in the future. While the legal and illegal acquisition of Western technology has helped bridge the gap in several significant areas, foreign technology cannot compensate for the general lack of innovative ability in the Soviet industrial sector. The lack of innovative capabilities throughout research and development and industrial elements will impede advances in civilian and military technology. The gap in manufacturing technologies is even more worrisome to the military because, despite its disproportionate share of assets, the defense industry is becoming more dependent on materials, components, and subassemblies supplied by the civilian economy. These shortcomings have led Soviet military leaders to express concern at least since the early 1980s about the economy's ability to support the development of future state-of-the-art weapons.

Metallurgy

The Soviets began a massive, well-coordinated, centrally directed effort shortly after World War II to become the world's largest ferrous and nonferrous metals producer. These metals were viewed as the keys to both military and industrial power. As a result of this effort, the Soviet Union is largely self-sufficient in most of these metals, even though they were often forced to exploit low-grade ores to avoid dependence on other countries. In many cases, they have developed a significant export potential.

Today, this manufacturing sector is reaching a critical period. Many of the key mines are becoming depleted, and the grade of ore is dropping. A large portion of the industrial plants are old, using inefficient equipment

40

and technology. Labor and power shortages, and a growing concern for the environment, are posing major constraints for Soviet metallurgical industries. The Soviets are turning to Western assistance to supply more efficient equipment and technology to enable them to continue the growth in output needed to sustain their economy.

Energy

Soviet industrial development has always been based in large part on vast amounts of relatively cheap resources — especially energy. The Soviets continue to be the world's largest producer of both oil and natural gas. Among the major industrial nations, the Soviet Union ranks number one in reserves of coal, natural gas, and oil. Older reserves, however, are becoming depleted and the Soviets have been exploiting reserves in less accessible areas of the USSR such as West Siberia. This is contributing to rising extraction costs which will lead to increases in overall energy costs. Despite rising costs, it will remain far cheaper for the USSR to produce oil domestically than to import it. Soviet oil exports, second only to those of Saudi Arabia, will remain profitable.

Energy conservation has been partially successful. Natural gas has displaced oil as the leader in the overall energy balance, thus improving energy efficiency and reducing environmental pollution.

Starting in the mid-1980s, the replacement of worn, energy-inefficient equipment became increasingly burdensome for the electric equipment industry. In addition, the post-Chernobyl cancellation of over 50 nuclear reactors further strained the electric equipment industry and prevented the planned replacement of conventional-fueled plants with nuclear plants. Electricity shortages appear inevitable after 1995 due to the stagnation of the nuclear energy program.

The USSR faces difficult near-term energy-related decisions particularly in the oil industry. Unless the Soviets continue to develop new reserves primarily with the help of imports of improved technology, oil output could decline, resulting in a partial loss of energy exports. This would diminish the country's leading source of hard-currency earnings. In the fuels and the electric power infrastructure, stagnation of the nuclear program further complicates the USSR's energy programs. Clearly, the Soviet economy cannot do without energy, and the USSR will probably be forced to make compromises among competing claimants for investment in energy industries and other equally pressing investment needs such as modernization, agriculture, housing, medicine,

transport, and defense.

Transport and Distribution

Soviet economic progress is being stifled by mounting problems in the transport and distribution system. The Soviet Union remains heavily reliant on rail transport for the distribution of raw materials and finished goods largely because roads are insufficiently developed in the USSR, particularly in rural areas. Soviet railroads, however, are plagued by inadequate construction, particularly of supporting infrastructure such as mechanized loading and unloading facilities, poor maintenance of existing rolling-stock, and a general lack of concern for safety. Railway managers are rewarded for total freight transported, leading to freight often traveling more kilometers than necessary, thereby clogging rail networks and resulting in spoilage of farm products.

Conversion

Soviet leaders seek to address the growing shortages in the civilian economy by redirecting resources and capacities released as a result of weapon production cuts into production of civilian goods. The leadership views the defense industry as the only sector with the available industrial capacity, raw materials, skilled labor, related experience, and effective management required to meet the tremendous needs of the civilian sector in the shortest time possible.

According to Soviet statements, some 400 defense plants and 100 civilian plants that produce military products are engaged in or are planning to become involved in industrial conversion. At least 200 military research and development organizations are said to be designing equipment and products needed in the civilian economy. The leadership has set 10 civilian production priorities for the defense industry which are key to Gorbachev's goals of raising living standards and modernizing the economy. Growth targets in these areas, however, appear grossly optimistic. The program met with difficulties in 1989, when even modest goals went unfulfilled. It is unlikely that plans to raise defense industry's civilian share of production from 40 percent in 1988 to 65 percent by 1995 will be achieved.

There is little enthusiasm in the defense sector for conversion. Defense industry officials resist being forced to produce civilian products unrelated to their current military production. In an effort to mute the impact on military production and preserve capacity for mobilization, defense industry officials are spreading conversion inefficiently among hundreds of plants. For the most part, conversion involves redirecting workers, raw ma-

CIVILIAN PRIORITIES FOR DEFENSE INDUSTRY

- **Food-Processing and Agricultural Equipment**
- **Textile Manufacturing Equipment**
- **Equipment for Public Catering Sector**
- **Consumer Goods**
- **Electronics**
- **Computer Equipment**
- **Medical Equipment**
- **Communications Equipment**
- **Civilian Aircraft and Equipment**
- **Civilian Fishing Vessels and Cargo Ships**

terials, and intermediate production resources toward existing civilian production. In other cases, new civilian product lines are set up using excess resources and idle capacity. In the instances where military production is being reduced, the military lines either continue to operate at lower rates, or some of a plant's production lines are being mothballed.

To date, the Soviets have designated only three defense-industry-subordinated plants for total conversion. All three plants — a shipyard and two ground forces equipment facilities — are only minor military producers that already produce more for the civilian economy than for defense. Closing facilities such as these will have no significant impact on the defense industry's ability to support the military in peace or war.

SOVIET MILITARY MANPOWER

Human resources are as critical to Soviet national power as industrial and technological resources, and are also a subject of increasing concern to the Soviet leadership. The predominantly Slavic European republics have experienced low birth rates and declining longevity while the traditionally Muslim regions — particularly the Central Asian republics — are seeing very high birth rates. The effect of these two trends has been a constraint on the overall population growth, a declining pool of new entrants into the labor force, and an altering of the USSR's ethnic composition. Ethnic Russians will soon lose their majority status in the population, although they will remain the dominant nationality. By 2010, they will comprise 40 percent of the population. Slavic nationalities — Russians as well as Ukrainians and Belorussians — will still constitute a majority through 2050, but Central Asian nationalities are expected to account for more than half the total population growth through 2010, and nearly two-thirds through 2050.

These demographic trends have sharpened the trade-offs in allocating entrants into the labor force throughout the various military, civilian, and university sectors of society. Because Soviet Muslims prefer to live in their home republics — where religious, cultural, and family ties are strong — population growth does little to relieve labor constraints in the European USSR, where Soviet military industry is concentrated. In the military, the declining proportion of Slavic nationalities has led to an increase in the conscription of non-Slavic nationalities.

The Soviet military press has published increasingly frank discussions of the manpower problems facing the armed forces. For example, educational levels among those from regions with significant Muslim populations remain uneven, with marked deficiencies in technical skills, particularly among conscripts from rural areas. Conscripts from Central Asian regions demonstrate lower proficiency than conscripts from Slavic regions in the use of sophisticated weapons and equipment. This lower proficiency is attributed primarily to their poor Russian language skills, which complicates training. The language barrier also complicates command by the officer corps, which is predominantly Slavic, and exacerbates discipline and morale problems in multiethnic military units. The declining proportion of Slavic conscripts, however, is leading to an increasing ethnic mix in combat units. Although the Soviets have implemented measures to improve Russian language instruction in Central Asian secondary schools and have attempted to recruit more Central Asians into the officer corps, neither strategy has enjoyed much success. This is due to the Central Asians' strong ethnic identification and resistance to assimilation into the predominantly Slavic culture. In fact, the Soviet military press reports that the number of draftees with poor knowledge of Russian is growing.

The December 1988 announcement of a 500,000-man reduction in military manpower could help reduce the military's reliance on non-Slavic — particularly Central Asian — minorities. The reductions will buy the Soviet leadership time to reassess the role of non-Russians in the armed forces, and to improve upon methods to encourage Muslim integration into the military. This respite, however, may be only temporary. The population's growth and changing ethnic composition will present challenges for Soviet leaders into the foreseeable future.

A 500,000-man reduction in the armed forces could help alleviate a number of other manpower-related problems, in addition to providing savings through reduced demand for weapon procurement and other military goods and services. The cut will provide unskilled labor to the civilian sector of the economy, supporting recent efforts to improve consumer welfare. According to the Soviets, the manpower reductions will include the release of 100,000 officers, many of whom possess engineering and technical skills required by Soviet industry.

Public involvement in military issues is threatening long-standing policies. A case in point is the military manning policy. The manpower system Gorbachev inherited was based on conscription. Soviet youth were introduced to military life in a mandatory premilitary training program, drafted at around age 18 for a mandatory two-year active-duty tour (three years in naval and KGB afloat units), assigned to mixed ethnic units far from home, and then discharged directly into the reserves, creating the massive mobilization base required by Soviet military doctrine.

This system is undergoing serious reappraisal, with an increasingly assertive Soviet public, particularly in the non-Russian republics, calling for wholesale reform of the military manning system. One set of proposals would modify the traditional policy of assigning conscripts far from home; activists from the Baltic and Caucasus republics, as well as Moldavia and the Ukraine, are pressuring the political leadership to station conscripts drafted from these republics closer to home.

Activists in several republics have gone farther by demanding that republic residents be exempt from service in the Soviet military and have drafted legislation on alternative service. In some cases, they advocate policies that would resurrect national units, analogous to those set up during the Russian Civil War. Other proposals would allow republics to set up their own armies and defense ministries. It is clear something must be done: between 1985 and 1989 incidents of draft evasion increased nearly eightfold, according to Soviet statements.

Despite adamant opposition from the high command (which has argued that giving republics their own armies or units would inflame already volatile interethnic disputes), the political leadership has signaled a willingness to negotiate on some of these demands. Some adjustments in the direction of home stationing were made during the fall 1989 call up of draftees, when up to a quarter of the draftees from selected republics (including the Baltic and Caucasus republics) were assigned to posts in their home military district. In the Caucasus, this policy complicated the Defense Ministry's mission of restoring order during the January 1990 flare-up of Azeri-Armenian violence by creating real and anticipated reliability problems with those indigenous minorities assigned to local units.

Further concessions to republic demands for home stationing or creation of national units would multiply the problems encountered in January and have major consequences for relations between Moscow and the republics, since such concessions may in effect endow republic authorities with their own military forces. It also would raise the question of how to procure manpower for those forces still deployed beyond Soviet borders and areas in the Soviet Union (such as the Far East) that have a limited conscription base.

Another series of proposals would introduce major changes in conscription policy. In spring 1989, the political leadership — over the strong objection of the high command — bowed to public pressure to reinstate student deferments, which had been gradually phased out in the early- and mid-1980s as the supply of draftees declined. In July 1989, also over military opposition, the deferment was applied retroactively to those students already drafted. Other proposals opposed by the military leadership would allow for alternative service for draft-eligibles who oppose participation in the military on religious or moral grounds. Another proposed change would decrease the service tenure from two years to one year. All these proposals would result in a decline in overall force levels.

Even more disturbing to the military leadership is the escalating political pressure to jettison the draft entirely in favor of a volunteer military. When it was first proposed, the military leadership was strongly opposed to the change, contending that the transition to what they call a "mercenary" army would be excessively expensive (because of the high salaries and perquisites needed to

---

PROBLEMS FACING RETURNING SOVIET SERVICEMEN

"The question of the withdrawal of Soviet troops from Czechoslovakia and Hungary is now acute. More than 35,000 officers and warrant officers and some 30,000 families will be returning to the motherland with them ... No one has given much thought to what this means. (The returning personnel) will virtually have the status of refugees, without apartments, their families without jobs, and their children (and there are nearly 19,000 of them) without schools."

Army General M.A. Moiseyev
Chief of the USSR Armed Forces General Staff
Krasnaya Zvezda, February 11, 1990

---

attract volunteers) and preclude the development of the large mobilization base of trained reservists that is still necessary because "the danger of war still exists." Since that time, there has been some small movement toward a professional military. Increased professionalism probably would result in a much smaller and more Slavic force due to Russian language requirements, as well as a probable lack of desire on the part of non-Slavs to volunteer because of cultural and nationalistic attitudes. This strategy also would entail a major expansion of the career enlisted contingent and noncommissioned officer corps as well as a major change in the mobilization system.

SOVIET MILITARY RESEARCH & DEVELOPMENT (R&D)

The Soviets have created an effective R&D base capable of developing equipment which, in some cases, is superior to Western systems in terms of militarily useful technology. The Soviet acquisition system accomplished this in spite of an uneven and, in many cases, backward technology base. The inefficiency of this system required the expenditure of a large amount of resources, which came at the expense of the overall economy. The Soviets now realize that their inefficient and increasingly backward economy will not support them adequately in countering Western high-technology weapon systems of the 1990s and beyond. This realization is a significant factor influencing the changes, from *perestroika* to troop reductions to new military doctrine, which are currently taking place.

Soviet military R&D is experiencing the effects of *perestroika* despite calls from military and civilian officials to spare it from budget cuts. The 1990 Soviet military R&D budget is targeted for 13.7 percent reduction, with further cuts possible in future budgets. While publicly released figures for the Soviet military R&D budget are assessed to significantly understate the full range and value of military R&D activity, the direction of change planned for the budget appears to indicate a real decline in military R&D spending. Military R&D budget cuts are occurring at a time when the Soviet Union is facing a vigorous technological challenge from the West and will certainly test the management skills of those in charge.

Continued research and development effectiveness in the face of these reductions will most likely come about by reducing inefficiencies in the system, eliminating duplicative research, and transferring some of the work to the civilian sector. More dramatic steps could include a halt in development of weapon systems that are not deemed essential for fulfillment of military requirements. The decision could also be made to skip the production of a generation of particular systems, concentrating on the less costly research phase to help produce a technologically superior product in the next generation. In addition, there is no evidence confirming that any major weapon development programs have been stretched out or canceled, and research and development of follow-on systems in all major weapon categories appear to be continuing with no sign of decline.

NOVOSTI/SOVFOTO

TASS/SOVFOTO

The deployment of the 20-ton *Kvant-2* module, shown here being prepared for launch to the *Mir* space station in late November 1989, vastly enhanced the Soviet space station's capabilities for military and scientific research.

From launch facilities such as Plesetsk, the Soviets continue to improve their military capabilities in space with the military space strategy of supporting terrestrial military forces and denying the use of space to other states.

44

Another effect of *perestroika* has been the diversion of some military resources to civilian applications. Military R&D facilities are being called on to increase their involvement in designing new civilian products. While the "conversion" of military R&D resources to civilian projects has apparently begun, Soviet officials complain that the pace is extremely slow. The emphasis on the technological advancement of the civil sector will hold some long-term advantages for military R&D despite the short-term constraints. The enhanced technological sophistication of the work force and the upgraded industrial infrastructure of the entire country will be supportive of future high-technology weapon systems.

Even in the short term there are certain benefits for military R&D. The dual-use nature of many of the 15 national priority technology programs (see inset) will clearly support the Soviet military along with the civilian sector. The work on future information technologies, advanced materials, and machine technology will all be of great importance to the military's renewed emphasis on improved utilization of technology for weapon systems, and better weapons' performance. This work will be aided by access to technology more easily transferred from the West as a result of Soviet reform efforts. Information technology advances will not only aid in the automated control and operation of individual weapon systems but will also be of great value to the Soviets for automated troop command and control. Advanced machine technology will make weapon system production more responsive, reduce the defense

NATIONAL PRIORITY TECHNOLOGY PROGRAMS

- High Energy Physics
- High Temperature Superconductivity
- Genetics
- Future Information Technologies
- Technologies, Machines, and Production of the Future
- Advanced Materials
- Advanced Biotechnology Methods
- High-Speed, Environmentally Clean Transport
- Environmentally Clean Energy Generation
- Resource-Saving and Environmentally Clean Production Processes in Metallurgy and Chemistry
- Efficient Food Production
- Fight Against Widespread Diseases
- Advanced Construction Technologies
- Exploration of Mars
- Controlled Thermonuclear Fusion

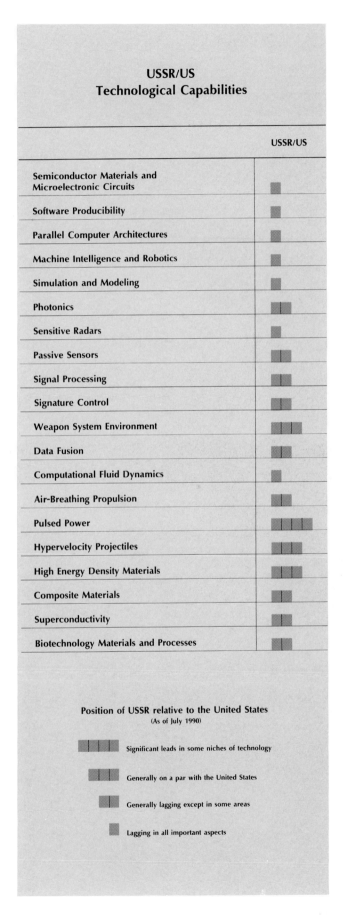

USSR/US Technological Capabilities

	USSR/US
Semiconductor Materials and Microelectronic Circuits	
Software Producibility	
Parallel Computer Architectures	
Machine Intelligence and Robotics	
Simulation and Modeling	
Photonics	
Sensitive Radars	
Passive Sensors	
Signal Processing	
Signature Control	
Weapon System Environment	
Data Fusion	
Computational Fluid Dynamics	
Air-Breathing Propulsion	
Pulsed Power	
Hypervelocity Projectiles	
High Energy Density Materials	
Composite Materials	
Superconductivity	
Biotechnology Materials and Processes	

Position of USSR relative to the United States
(As of July 1990)

Significant leads in some niches of technology

Generally on a par with the United States

Generally lagging except in some areas

Lagging in all important aspects

Relative USSR/US Technology Level in Deployed Military Systems[1]

DEPLOYED SYSTEMS	US SUPERIOR	US/USSR EQUAL	USSR SUPERIOR
STRATEGIC			
ICBMs		■	
SSBNs	■		
SLBMs	■➤		
Bombers	■		
SAMs			■
Ballistic Missile Defense			■
Antisatellite			■
Cruise Missiles	■		
TACTICAL			
Land Forces			
SAMs (Including Naval)		■➤	
Tanks		■➤	
Artillery		■➤	
Infantry Combat Vehicles		■➤	
Antitank Guided Missiles		■➤	
Attack Helicopters	■➤		
Chemical Warfare			■
Biological Warfare[2]			■
Air Forces			
Fighter/Attack and Interceptor Aircraft	■➤		
Air-to-Air Missiles	■➤		

DEPLOYED SYSTEMS	US SUPERIOR	US/USSR EQUAL	USSR SUPERIOR
Air-to-Surface Munitions	■➤		
Airlift Aircraft	■➤		
Naval Forces			
SSNs	■➤		
Torpedoes		■	
Sea-Based Aircraft	■		
Surface Combatants	■		
Naval Cruise Missiles		■➤	
Mines		■	
C^3I			
Communications	■➤		
ECM/ECCM	■➤		
Early Warning	■➤		
Surveillance and Reconnaissance	■➤		
Training Simulators	■		

The arrows denote that the relative technology level is changing significantly in the direction indicated.

Relative comparisons of deployed technology levels shown depict overall average standing; countries may be superior, equal, or inferior in subsystems of a specific technology in deployed military system.

[1] These are comparisons of system technology levels only, and are not necessarily a measure of effectiveness. The comparisons are not dependent on scenario, tactics, quantity, training, or other operational factors. Systems farther than one year from IOC are not considered.

[2] The United States has no deployed biological warfare systems.

As of September 1990

burden on the economy, and allow for faster, more cost-effective incorporation of new materials into these weapon systems.

TECHNOLOGICAL COMPETITION

The time delay between the initiation of pure research and the application of the resultant technology to a military system typically is about 20 to 30 years. The Soviets understand this and have a long history of supporting research activities. Soviet military writers ascribe revolutionary military potential to the emerging generation of military technologies and decry the technological weaknesses of the Soviet economy. Nevertheless, the Soviet Union remains a formidable technological power and is striving to improve its defense technological base. The recent changes in the political and economic structure of Europe will not change this fundamental Soviet dedication to research and development of militarily applicable technologies or the acquisition of these technologies through technology transfer or espionage.

The Soviet Union is currently lagging behind the US, but actively researching air-breathing propulsion, biotechnology materials and processes, composite materials, data fusion, passive sensors, photonics, and signal processing. They are on par with the US in the critical technology areas of high energy density materials and hypervelocity projectiles. It is envisaged that they will continue to exploit our open scientific literature, technical exchange programs fostered by the spirit of *glasnost,* and espionage to accelerate their research in these militarily critical areas. They are significantly ahead of the US in the area of pulsed power that enables the development and production of directed energy weapons, kinetic energy weapons, target identification, and surveillance systems. These technologies have significant applications in the field of antisatellite weaponry. This field requires advanced technological capability in the form of energy storage, pulse-forming networks, and coupling of the pulse-to-load as in laser and high-power microwave applications. The direct military application of these technologies is in the areas of high-power microwaves, electrothermal guns, electromagnetic launchers, neutral particle beam systems, a variety of lasers, charged particle beams, and ultra-wide band radars. These technologies will have significant impact in the commercial areas of electrical power generation, electric drives and controls, and within the medical industry.

PROSPECTS

The choices Soviet leaders make in the near future on resource allocation and economic reform likely will determine their future superpower status. Resource reallocation through defense budget cuts and conversion are likely to continue over the next few years. These efforts alone, however, are not a panacea for overcoming the ills of the Soviet economy and will be insufficient to overcome the inertia of the existing system. Without reforming the existing command economic system into a more efficient market-driven system, reallocation schemes run the substantial risk of becoming yet additional ineffective half-measures that seal *perestroika's* fate in the system's ingrained economic inefficiencies.

To date, however, the Soviet leadership appears incapable of carrying out the comprehensive reforms to bring about the fundamental economic changes necessary to raise productivity and restore growth. Until the Soviets are prepared to dismantle the failed command economy, embrace market mechanisms, and accept the initial high costs of unemployment and rising prices, the economy has little reasonable hope for recovery. Without systemic reform, the Soviet Union is assured of continued economic decline and instability. Even if radical reforms are adopted, the Soviets face many years of economic turmoil before they can hope to see significant improvements.

The paradox remains, however, that in spite of these increasing economic difficulties, the Soviets are continuing to fund expensive military research and development activities and produce technologically advanced weapon systems. Such spending will continue to come at the expense of the civilian sector.

Nuclear, Strategic Defense, and Space Programs and the US-Soviet Balance

TASS, SOVFOTO

The continued modernization of Soviet strategic forces, including the deployment of land attack cruise missiles on the Blackjack bomber and submarines, will preserve Soviet capabilities to support a warfighting doctrine.

INTRODUCTION

Soviet strategic forces and nuclear policy are changing, but thus far the changes are less dramatic than those occurring in other areas of Soviet policy. The Soviets assert that Western nuclear forces present the primary external military threat to the Soviet Union. Moscow,

therefore, considers modernization essential, both in response to changing capabilities of potential adversaries and to internal political realities which pressure for a force structure that is leaner, yet still capable of meeting the requirements for waging strategic nuclear war.

This chapter focuses on those critical forces which

together influence the shape of the strategic balance. An understanding of Soviet views on nuclear war, combined with knowledge of force structure and the interrelationship between the components of Soviet strategic power, will allow for a more balanced assessment of the threat facing the United States. The first section of the chapter examines Soviet strategic, theater, and short-range nuclear forces. This is followed by a discussion of active and passive strategic defenses, radio-electronic combat (REC), and finally, space forces and their role in support of the Soviet Union's warfighting capability. The section concludes with prospects for change in Soviet nuclear, strategic defense, and space capabilities. The second portion of this chapter evaluates the US-Soviet strategic balance of forces through a presentation of various measures of military power.

NUCLEAR FORCES

This section includes a discussion of Soviet strategic offensive, theater, and short-range nuclear forces. Nuclear weapons that are part of Soviet strategic antiballistic missile defense systems are discussed in the section on strategic defenses.

Strategic Nuclear Forces

Strategic Missions and Operations

The Soviets appear to assess that a future war would develop out of a period of major international tension and crisis. In the Soviet assessment, some nuclear assets, including theater nuclear weapons and Soviet ballistic missile submarines, in particular, would be lost to conventional attacks during the initial phase of the war. In the Soviet perception, a future war waged for decisive objectives likely would eventually escalate to the nuclear level. A major Soviet military theorist, Army-General M. A. Gareyev, now Deputy Chief of the General Staff, wrote in the late 1980s that "neither of the sides possessing nuclear weapons will permit its defeat in a conventional war without having resorted to nuclear weapons."

The Soviet Union has declared continually since 1982 that it will not be the first nation to use nuclear weapons under any circumstances, but their forces have the capability to conduct a first strike. Should Soviet intelligence predict an imminent nuclear attack, the Soviets likely would try to pre-empt an enemy strike with a massive strategic nuclear strike. In spite of dramatic policy changes and declaration of a new defensive doctrine, the Soviets continue to maintain a capability to execute a pre-emptive nuclear strike.

Should they fail to pre-empt, the Soviets perceive that they may have to launch a nuclear strike while under attack. To deal with this contingency, they have deployed a missile attack warning system of launch detection satellites, over-the-horizon radars, and large phased-array radars (LPARs) that can provide the Soviet high command with up to 30 minutes' warning of an intercontinental ballistic missile (ICBM) attack.

Soviet military theorists traditionally have held that the initial nuclear exchange will likely decide the course and ultimate outcome of the conflict. However, they acknowledge that a period of protracted nuclear operations may be required before war termination. To ensure effective nuclear operations during such a phase, the Soviets continue to take extensive preparatory measures.

- They have designed their nuclear force command and control system for maximum survivability. It combines hardened command posts, redundant communications means, and ground- and air-mobile command and communication assets.
- They have deployed increasing numbers of road- and rail-mobile launchers in the Strategic Rocket Forces (SRF).
- They have staged airfields for long-range bomber survivability, and logistical sites for nuclear-powered ballistic missile submarines (SSBNs) to support force reconstitution.
- They have equipped their strategic forces with a reload and refire capability.

The Soviet Supreme High Command coordinates wartime employment of the SRF, the Navy's ballistic missile and strategic land-attack cruise missile submarines, and Long Range Aviation (LRA) intercontinental strike assets into a single, integrated nuclear strike operation. During a war, the General Headquarters (or Stavka) of the Armed Forces' Supreme High

Stavka of the Soviet Supreme High Command - 1990

C-in-C Soviet Armed Forces

M.S. Gorbachev

Minister of Defense

D.T. Yazov

Chief of Main Political Directorate

N.I. Shlyaga

No Photo Available

First Deputy Minister of Defense

M.A. Moiseyev (Chief of the General Staff)

First Deputy Minister of Defense

P.G. Lushev (C-in-C Warsaw Pact Forces)

First Deputy Minister of Defense

K.A. Kochetov

Deputy Minister of Defense

V.I. Varennikov (C-in-C Ground Forces)

Deputy Minister of Defense

Y.P. Maksimov (C-in-C Strategic Rocket Forces)

Deputy Minister of Defense

I.M. Tret'yak (C-in-C Air Defense Forces)

Deputy Minister of Defense

Y.I. Shaposhnikov (C-in-C Air Forces)

Deputy Minister of Defense

V.N. Chernavin (C-in-C Naval Forces)

Stavka Personnel-1985

C-in-C Soviet Armed Forces

M.S. Gorbachev

Minister of Defense

S.L. Sokolov

Chief of Main Political Directorate

A.A. Yepishev

First Deputy Minister of Defense

S.F. Akhromeyev (Chief of the General Staff)

First Deputy Minister of Defense

V.G. Kulikov (C-in-C Warsaw Pact Forces)

First Deputy Minister of Defense

V.I. Petrov

Deputy Minister of Defense

Y.F. Ivanovskiy (C-in-C Ground Forces)

Deputy Minister of Defense

V.F. Tolubko (C-in-C Strategic Rocket Forces)

Deputy Minister of Defense

A.I. Koldunov (C-in-C Air Defense Forces)

Deputy Minister of Defense

A.N. Yefimov (C-in-C Air Forces)

Deputy Minister of Defense

S.G. Gorshkov (C-in-C Naval Forces)

As of August 1990

Command (VGK) would directly control the strategic nuclear forces through the General Staff's Main Operations Directorate.

Strategic Nuclear Forces Developments

The Soviets are conducting a comprehensive modernization program and, although they are structuring this program in anticipation of reductions under a Strategic Arms Reduction Talks (START) Treaty, it will result in a force that is more accurate, survivable, and reliable.

The Soviet nuclear forces include ICBMs under the operational control of the SRF, submarine-launched ballistic missiles (SLBMs) deployed aboard SSBNs, and cruise missile-armed strategic intercontinental bombers as part of LRA. The Soviets are modernizing all three legs of their forces.

By the end of this decade, particularly after a START Treaty is implemented, the composition of Soviet strategic forces will change significantly. The proportion of mobile ICBM launchers likely will increase to about two-thirds the total ICBM force, giving the Soviets a more survivable force. Heavy ICBMs will continue to carry about half of the warheads, despite reductions in the number of launchers. This force structure, together with ongoing improvements to the SS-18, will enable the Soviets to retain a credible hard-target-kill capability against US Minuteman and Peacekeeper silos. The Soviets are destroying older ICBMs as new ones are deployed; thus by the end of the decade they will be left with the SS-18, SS-24 Mods 1 and 2, the SS-25, and their follow-ons. The size of the SSBN force will decline by nearly one-third, and the number of SLBM warheads will decrease slightly. The operational bomber force will not grow substantially, but it will be modernized as more air-launched cruise-missile (ALCM)-carrying bombers

enter the force. The percentage of ICBM and SLBM launchers within the strategic nuclear forces will decline slightly under a START Treaty, while the percentage of bombers will rise. The percentage of warheads carried on bombers will rise relative to ICBMs and SLBMs.

The Soviets are maintaining continuity in their strategic nuclear forces through an aggressive program of strategic nuclear force modernization. Because of the retirement of older systems, the number of strategic delivery systems is decreasing for the first time. The number of warheads, however, is remaining about the same, at least for the near term.

Strategic Rocket Forces Developments

The Soviet Union is comprehensively modernizing its ICBM force. Although the pace is not as rapid as previous modernization programs of the 1970s and early 1980s, nonetheless it will produce a formidable force that is highly capable and more survivable and flexible than its predecessors. Soviet perceptions of an eventual START Treaty appear to be dictating the scope and pace of their SRF modernization program.

Current Soviet ICBM modernization has three aspects: the continued deployment of two new missiles — the SS-24 [in both a rail-mobile (Mod 1) and silo (Mod 2) version], and the road-mobile SS-25; the modernization of the SS-18 heavy ICBM (Mod 5 and Mod 6); and the corresponding removal of older missile systems.

A centerpiece of the modernization program is the emphasis on survivability through the infusion of mobility into the force structure. The Soviets currently have several garrisons for the rail-mobile SS-24 ICBM. This system can roam most of the Soviet rail network, which consists of more than 145,000 kilometers of broad-gauge

Modernization of the Soviet Strategic Rocket Forces with more capable systems continues apace. Three new or upgraded ICBMs, the SS-18 Mod 5, SS-24, and SS-25, are being deployed and will constitute the ICBM leg of the Soviet strategic nuclear forces under START.

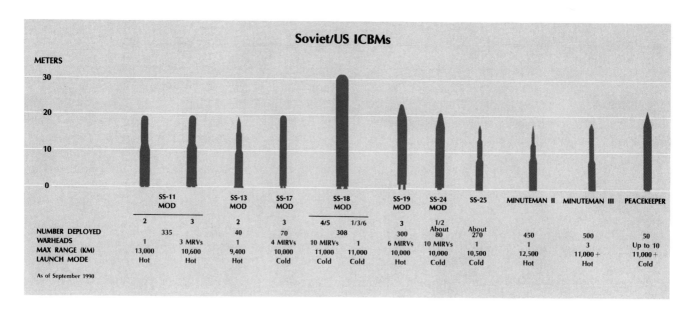

Soviet/US ICBMs

	SS-11 MOD		SS-13 MOD	SS-17 MOD	SS-18 MOD		SS-19 MOD	SS-24 MOD	SS-25	MINUTEMAN II	MINUTEMAN III	PEACEKEEPER
	2	3			4/5	1/3/6	3	1/2				
NUMBER DEPLOYED	335		40	70	308		300	About 80	About 270	450	500	50
WARHEADS	1	3 MRVs	1	4 MIRVs	10 MIRVs	1	6 MIRVs	10 MIRVs	1	1	3	Up to 10
MAX RANGE (KM)	13,000	10,600	9,400	10,000	11,000	11,000	10,000	10,000	10,500	12,500	11,000 +	11,000 +
LAUNCH MODE	Hot	Hot	Hot	Cold	Cold	Cold	Hot	Cold	Cold	Hot	Hot	Cold

As of September 1990

track. The military is involved in all aspects of railroad operations and, in spite of recent rail network problems, would ensure the highest priority is given to the SS-24 train on all routes. The broad area available for deployment of both the SS-24 and SS-25 mobile systems and the use of concealment measures would complicate locating these systems in wartime. Since 1985, the Soviets have deployed about 290 mobile ICBMs. Deployments probably will continue at a brisk pace. The mobile SS-24 and SS-25 will likely comprise about two-thirds of total ICBM launchers in the future. It appears that most operational SS-25 deployments in the future will occur at former SS-20 intermediate-range ballistic missile (IRBM) bases which have been eliminated under the Intermediate-Range Nuclear Forces (INF) Treaty.

Silo conversion activity is currently under way to replace older variants of the SS-18 — the bulwark of the SRF hard-target-kill capability — with more capable versions. These include the SS-18 Mod 5 [with substantially more accuracy and warhead yield and equipped with multiple independently-targetable reentry vehicles (MIRVs)], and the single-warhead Mod 6. The Soviets are modernizing their SS-18 force with START constraints in mind, requiring a 50-percent cut in heavy ICBMs. Despite this limitation, improvements in the Mod 5's accuracy and yield will allow the Soviets to maintain a credible wartime hard-target-kill capability.

The Soviets also have converted over 50 SS-19 silos to the new SS-24 Mod 2 system. This program appears nearly complete and likely will be only a small portion of the ICBM force. The SS-24 is a solid-propellant system, intended for use against soft or semihardened targets. The Soviets also continue to draw down older silo-based systems, such as the SS-11, SS-13, and SS-17 ICBMs,

in compensation. Eventually, the Soviets probably will destroy the remaining 300 SS-19 silos not converted to support the SS-24 Mod 2. By eliminating these silo-based systems the Soviets are streamlining their ICBM force and giving it a decidedly mobile character.

The removal of older missiles will create a more consolidated force, reducing the number of ICBM missile types from the seven currently deployed to just three or four by the mid-to-late 1990s. With the three ICBM systems currently being deployed, the Soviets have the flexibility to adjust their force composition over the next few years. Should the START process be interrupted, the Soviets could resume their modernization efforts without regard to START limits.

Strategic Aviation Force Developments

The Soviet intercontinental bomber force continues to modernize, enhancing its role in Soviet nuclear forces. New Bear H and Blackjack aircraft equipped with long-range ALCMs continue to be introduced into the Soviet bomber fleet. With the retirement of older bomb- and missile-carrying Bear aircraft, about three-fourths of the

New Bear H and Blackjack aircraft equipped with long-range ALCMs continue to be introduced into the Soviet bomber fleet.

TASS/SOVFOTO

Soviet post-START bomber force will consist of modern ALCM-equipped aircraft.

The continued production of modern Midas tankers improves the in-flight refueling support available to Soviet bombers. Staging from bases in the Arctic region or refueling in-flight, Bear H bombers can put all of Canada and the United States within range of their missiles.

A post-START bomber force will reflect an ongoing program of modernization as the Soviets remove obsolete bombers from their force and replace them with ALCM-carrying bombers. The prominence of ALCM-equipped aircraft will give the Soviet bomber force an enhanced strategic strike capability.

SSBN/SLBM Developments

Recent SSBN force developments are consistent with the trend toward a more streamlined and highly capable strategic nuclear force that will present an increasingly lethal threat. With 63 total platforms, the Soviet SSBN force accounts for about 30 percent of available strategic nuclear warheads. Thirteen of the most modern, capable platforms (Delta IVs and Typhoons) carry MIRVed, long-range SLBMs that eventually may have a hard-target-kill potential against targets in the continental United States.

As older, less-capable ballistic missile platforms, like Yankee SSBNs, are phased out, newer, more survivable platforms with qualitative upgrades in both the missile and platform systems are entering the fleet. The Soviets added one Delta IV and one Typhoon SSBN to the inventory in 1989, and launched a seventh Delta IV in early 1990. This upgrade trend will result in a generally more efficient and ready strategic navy.

Soviet SSBNs can strike targets worldwide while on patrol in well-defended SSBN bastion areas near the Soviet Union. Combined-arms groupings of air, surface, and subsurface antisubmarine warfare (ASW) assets are allocated to ensure SSBN survivability during wartime. Improvements made during the 1980s in SSBN communications, SLBM warhead lethality, and SSBN survivability ensure that the capabilities and importance of this force will increase in the future.

Cruise Missile Developments

The Soviet Union has two nuclear-capable, long-range cruise missile systems — the AS-15/Kent ALCM and the SS-N-21/Sampson sea-launched cruise missile (SLCM). The Soviets deploy the AS-15 on Bear H and Blackjack intercontinental bombers. The 3,000 kilometer stand-off range of the AS-15 ALCM allows their launch outside US or Canadian airspace. Two new land-attack, long-range cruise missiles, the AS-X-19 and the SS-NX-24, are under development and the AS-X-19 may reach initial operational capability in the early 1990s. Their introduction into Long Range Aviation and submarine forces would add potent weapons to the Soviet inventory and reflects the continuing trend toward modernization in the ALCM-equipped bomber force and subsurface fleet. The SS-N-21 probably can be launched from any appropriately modified modern nuclear-powered general purpose submarine and probably would be used primarily against Eurasian theater strategic targets. Specific candidates for employment are Yankee Notch-, Akula-, and possibly Victor III- and Sierra-class nuclear-powered attack submarines (SSNs).

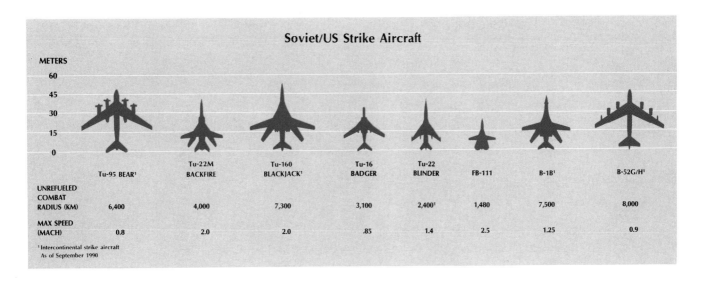

Soviet/US Strike Aircraft

	Tu-95 BEAR[1]	Tu-22M BACKFIRE	Tu-160 BLACKJACK[1]	Tu-16 BADGER	Tu-22 BLINDER	FB-111	B-1B[1]	B-52G/H[1]
UNREFUELED COMBAT RADIUS (KM)	6,400	4,000	7,300	3,100	2,400[1]	1,480	7,500	8,000
MAX SPEED (MACH)	0.8	2.0	2.0	.85	1.4	2.5	1.25	0.9

[1] Intercontinental strike aircraft
As of September 1990

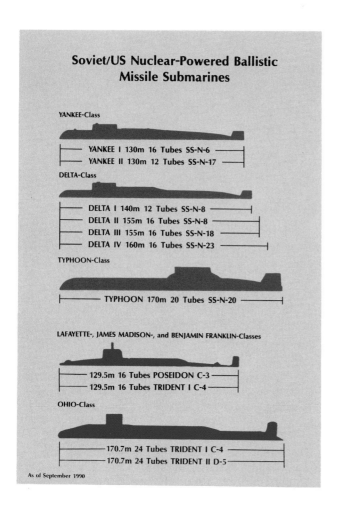

Soviet/US Nuclear-Powered Ballistic Missile Submarines

YANKEE-Class

YANKEE I 130m 16 Tubes SS-N-6
YANKEE II 130m 12 Tubes SS-N-17

DELTA-Class

DELTA I 140m 12 Tubes SS-N-8
DELTA II 155m 16 Tubes SS-N-8
DELTA III 155m 16 Tubes SS-N-18
DELTA IV 160m 16 Tubes SS-N-23

TYPHOON-Class

TYPHOON 170m 20 Tubes SS-N-20

LAFAYETTE-, JAMES MADISON-, and BENJAMIN FRANKLIN-Classes

129.5m 16 Tubes POSEIDON C-3
129.5m 16 Tubes TRIDENT I C-4

OHIO-Class

170.7m 24 Tubes TRIDENT I C-4
170.7m 24 Tubes TRIDENT II D-5

As of September 1990

As part of their ongoing development programs, the Soviets likely will integrate advancing technologies like enhanced ranges, lower radar cross-sections, and conventional munitions into their new cruise missiles.

Prospects

The Soviets will continue to modernize systematically their strategic offensive forces, maintaining a trend toward improved force lethality, responsiveness, and survivability. Despite the decline in the threat of a short-warning ground attack against NATO, the US cannot ignore the Soviet capability to launch a short-warning or pre-emptive strategic nuclear attack against the continental United States for the foreseeable future — although such an attack is judged to be unlikely.

The direction of Soviet strategic nuclear force development will continue to be driven primarily by Soviet strategic warfighting requirements, particularly the preferred type of strike, targeting philosophy, perceived emerging US capabilities, and future arms control requirements. Modernization of the bomber force, coupled with the emerging hard-target-kill capability of

the SLBM force and the increasing number of mobile ICBMs, will give the Soviets a more balanced and survivable strategic nuclear force structure.

The direction and pace of Soviet strategic force modernization will also be strongly influenced by any US decision to deploy a strategic defense system. The USSR will invest heavily in systems and technology to maintain the offensive capability of its strategic nuclear forces. The Soviets could attempt to counter a US strategic defense system by deploying large numbers of warheads to saturate US sensors (thereby abrogating the START Treaty) or maneuvering reentry vehicles to evade defenses. They could also employ penetration aids, antisatellite weapons, and fast-burn boosters. They have implied that future strategic arms control agreements depend on continued observance of limits on strategic defenses.

Theater Nuclear Forces

There have been dramatic reductions in Soviet theater forces. The terms of the INF Treaty require the elimination of the Soviets' deployed and non-deployed intermediate-range nuclear systems — the road-transportable SS-4 medium-range ballistic missile (MRBM) and road-mobile SS-20 IRBM. These systems provided the USSR the capability to attack European nonhardened targets.

The Soviets have eliminated over three-quarters of the SS-20 force of 654 launchers, and no SS-4s or SS-5s remain. The remainder of SS-20s will be eliminated in less than a year, as the Treaty mandates June 1991 as the completion date for destruction.

Even after INF and anticipated START Treaty reductions, the Soviets likely will continue to effectively satisfy their critical theater targeting requirements by means of their existing nuclear-capable aircraft as well as through the ongoing modernization of their strategic forces. ICBMs and SLBMs, supplemented by aviation assets, can cover former SS-20 targets. The SS-11 and SS-19 ICBMs, until their destruction under the START Treaty, and all SLBMs deployed in Soviet-protected bastions, can provide target coverage, with SS-24s and SS-25s potentially available as well.

Short-Range Nuclear Forces (SNF)

Short-range nuclear forces (SNF) are those forces possessing nuclear-capable weapon systems that have a range of 500 kilometers or less. Soviet short-range nuclear forces consist of short-range ballistic missiles (SRBMs) (SS-1, Scud, and SS-21 Scarab), rockets

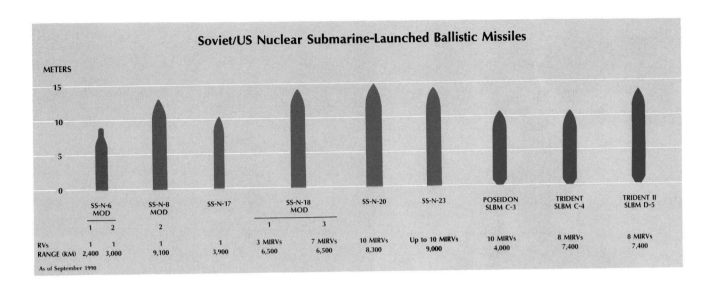

Soviet/US Nuclear Submarine-Launched Ballistic Missiles

	SS-N-6 MOD		SS-N-8 MOD	SS-N-17	SS-N-18 MOD		SS-N-20	SS-N-23	POSEIDON SLBM C-3	TRIDENT SLBM C-4	TRIDENT II SLBM D-5
	1	2	2		1	3					
RVs	1	1	1	1	3 MIRVs	7 MIRVs	10 MIRVs	Up to 10 MIRVs	10 MIRVs	8 MIRVs	8 MIRVs
RANGE (KM)	2,400	3,000	9,100	3,900	6,500	6,500	8,300	9,000	4,000	7,400	7,400

As of September 1990

(FROG-7), and nuclear-capable artillery (152-mm, 203-mm, and 240-mm).

Soviet force reorganization, force withdrawals, proposed Conventional Armed Forces in Europe (CFE) reductions, and the doctrine of "reasonable sufficiency," will diminish the capability of Soviet theater forces to conduct nuclear operations in Europe. It should be noted, however, that the importance of theater nuclear forces in Soviet strategy has not decreased, and that short-range nuclear forces withdrawn to Soviet territory remain within the Western Theater of Operations. In addition, the Soviets might not remove all of the nuclear warheads accompanying such forces until very late in the process of their withdrawal. In early June 1990, Soviet Foreign Minister Shevardnadze announced that the Soviets will remove 1,500 nuclear warheads from Eastern Europe. The weapons withdrawn will probably be transferred to the western Soviet Union and will remain readily available to nuclear forces remaining in Eastern Europe or those based in the USSR.

Currently, the Soviet Union possesses more than 1,400 SRBM launchers, all capable of delivering nuclear weapons. The Soviet Union's SNF modernization program includes replacing FROG rocket launchers with SS-21 short-range ballistic missiles organized into brigades of 18 launchers each. This improved organizational structure increases flexibility and responsiveness; it also simplifies command and control. The command and control processes for these forces are also being automated, greatly improving their capabilities.

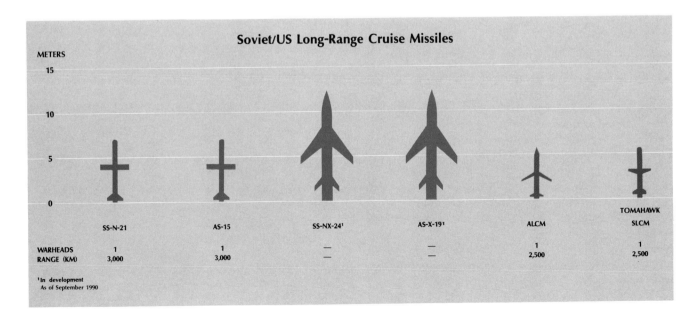

Soviet/US Long-Range Cruise Missiles

	SS-N-21	AS-15	SS-NX-24[1]	AS-X-19[1]	ALCM	TOMAHAWK SLCM
WARHEADS	1	1	—	—	1	1
RANGE (KM)	3,000	3,000	—	—	2,500	2,500

[1] In development
As of September 1990

The Typhoon ballistic missile submarine carries 20 SLBMs that will eventually have a hard-target-kill potential against the continental United States. The Soviets added the sixth and final Typhoon to the inventory in 1989.

The Soviets also have embarked on a modernization program for their artillery assets, replacing older, towed systems with improved self-propelled versions. At the same time, force structure changes that are reducing the size of the artillery force are also taking place. The Soviet military is decreasing artillery batteries from six or eight guns to four guns throughout the force. These changes result in qualitative improvements in Soviet artillery at the division level.

While the Soviet Union is undertaking many changes in its short-range nuclear forces, the net result will be a more modern and efficient force. The force structure changes taking place throughout the ground forces will have an effect on the composition and operation of short-range nuclear systems organic to ground forces elements. Reductions in numbers will be at least partially offset by improvements in the delivery systems themselves. In the future, the Soviet SNF probably will be a smaller, improved and formidable force, possessing the capability to conduct extensive nuclear operations.

STRATEGIC DEFENSE

Missions and Operations

The Soviets view active and passive strategic defense as critical components of a nuclear strategy dedicated to limiting wartime damage to the Soviet Union. The variety of weapon systems fielded or in development and the scope of their active and passive defense capabilities illustrate their strong and continuing commitment to strategic defense programs. The Soviets have fielded extensive strategic air defenses, upgrading them with multi-engagement surface-to-air missile units, advanced (fourth-generation) fighter-interceptors, computer-assisted command and control systems, and modern three-dimensional radars.

They also have upgraded Moscow's antiballistic missile (ABM) system into a dual-layered system. Research and development (R&D) efforts continue in traditional and advanced ABM technologies. The Soviets' extensive program of passive defense measures — including civil defense, mobility, hardening, and redundancy — is intended to limit the effects of enemy nuclear strikes on Soviet territory.

Funding support for strategic defense programs, as a percentage of Soviet military spending, continues to show a long-term commitment. Current political pressures and economic problems, however, are forcing somewhat slower deployment of strategic defense weapons, and some reductions in air defense forces have been announced.

The loss of Soviet air defense facilities in East European countries will degrade air defense of the Soviet Union, as these countries provide primarily a defensive buffer zone against air attacks originating from NATO territories. However, the most recent meeting of the Warsaw Pact left air defense under unified command for the immediate future. The Soviets believe that if they relinquish air defense facilities in the Baltic states, the effect on their air defense would be significant. Loss of these facilities would severely limit early warning radar coverage at low altitude and decrease reaction times available to interceptor aircraft. It would also open a serious gap in their ballistic missile early warning coverage.

Active Defenses

Antiballistic Missile (ABM) Defense

In 1989, the new Soviet ABM system around Moscow became operational. The new system provides Moscow with dual-layer defensive coverage against ballistic missile attack. Its components are the Gazelle and modified Galosh interceptors, and the multifunctional Pill Box radar at Pushkino, north of Moscow.

The modified Galosh is a silo-launched missile for exoatmospheric or high-altitude, long-range intercepts. The Gazelle is a high performance silo-launched missile designed to intercept reentry vehicles in the atmosphere that leak through the outer layer of defense. The Pill Box is a large, four-sided phased-array radar with 360-degree coverage which controls these new interceptors. Its many antenna elements permit the user to rapidly direct the radar beams with a high degree of tracking accuracy. While the new system apparently will comprise the full 100 launchers permitted by the 1972 ABM Treaty, it has major weaknesses. The limited number of launchers and reliance on the single Pill Box radar limits the overall effectiveness of the system, although it does provide a defense against a limited attack or accidental launch.

The Soviets are continuing extensive research and development efforts in both traditional and advanced technologies for ballistic missile defense. In the late 1960s, the USSR initiated a substantial research program into advanced technologies applicable to ballistic missile defense systems. As noted by Gorbachev in 1987, this effort covers many of the same technologies being explored by the US Strategic Defense Initiative. The Soviet effort, however, involves a much greater investment of plant space, capital, and manpower.

Missile Attack Warning System

In the mid-1970s, the Soviets began building a network of large phased-array radars (LPARs). Moscow's recognition of the Krasnoyarsk radar as a violation of the 1972 ABM Treaty and environmental activism within the Soviet Union both have adversely affected the LPAR construction program, and it is unclear whether the complete network of LPARs will be deployed as planned. Following long-standing complaints by the United States that Krasnoyarsk violated the ABM Treaty because of its orientation and location in the interior of the Soviet Union, the Soviets acknowledged the violation and agreed to dismantle the LPAR. Dismantlement has already begun. In addition, Defense Minister Dmitriy Yazov has announced that construction at the nearly completed LPAR at Mukachevo, near the Ukrainian-Hungarian border, has been temporarily halted. With the dismantlement of Krasnoyarsk, the Soviets will continue to have a gap in coverage in the northeast.

Aviation of Air Defense (APVO)

Soviet Aviation of Air Defense (APVO) has continued to improve its capability to defend the Soviet homeland against air attack. The Soviets continue to replace older fighter-interceptors with modern fourth-generation aircraft that have longer ranges, can carry larger payloads, and have advanced, look-down shoot-down capabilites. To date, fourth-generation aircraft provide about one-fourth of the current APVO inventory. Modern Flanker and Foxhound units have replaced all obsolete Fiddler and Firebar regiments in the USSR.

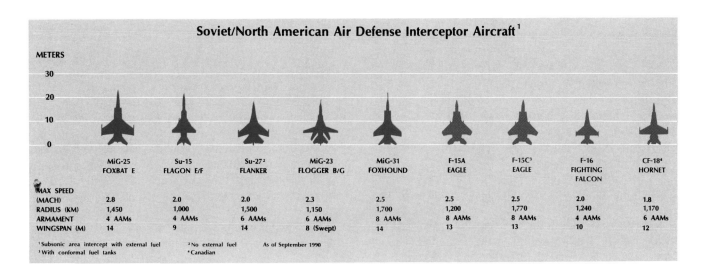

Soviet/North American Air Defense Interceptor Aircraft[1]

METERS	MiG-25 FOXBAT E	Su-15 FLAGON E/F	Su-27[2] FLANKER	MiG-23 FLOGGER B/G	MiG-31 FOXHOUND	F-15A EAGLE	F-15C[3] EAGLE	F-16 FIGHTING FALCON	CF-18[4] HORNET
MAX SPEED (MACH)	2.8	2.0	2.0	2.3	2.5	2.5	2.5	2.0	1.8
RADIUS (KM)	1,450	1,000	1,500	1,150	1,700	1,200	1,770	1,240	1,170
ARMAMENT	4 AAMs	4 AAMs	6 AAMs	6 AAMs	8 AAMs	8 AAMs	8 AAMs	4 AAMs	6 AAMs
WINGSPAN (M)	14	9	14	8 (Swept)	14	13	13	10	12

[1] Subsonic area intercept with external fuel   [2] No external fuel   As of September 1990
[3] With conformal fuel tanks   [4] Canadian

Soviet deployment of their sophisticated Mainstay Airborne Warning and Control System (AWACS) aircraft slowed recently with only one additional Mainstay deployed to the APVO inventory in 1989. The Mainstay continues to work with APVO fighters to project homeland air defenses well beyond the borders of the USSR.

The steady deployment of fourth-generation interceptors into the force has been accompanied by a reduction of the average regiment size of the new aircraft by six to nine aircraft, reducing the total interceptor inventory. Concurrently, APVO's ability to engage low-altitude targets with more weapons and for a longer time has improved greatly.

Command, Control, and Communications (C³)

The Soviets have dedicated a great amount of time and effort to streamline and update air defense command, control, and communications (C³). Successful air defense operations depend greatly on speed, efficiency, and reliability of communications. Newer, more integrated air defense C³ systems enhance early warning and target handling capability. Passive detection systems located on the country's periphery help the air surveillance network improve early warning capability. The Soviets also make extensive use of computer-assisted decisionmaking equipment including air defense battle management systems and more efficient, redundant communications systems.

Radio-Electronic Combat (REC)

Soviet planners use the term REC to refer to their program to disrupt enemy command and control. REC doctrine embodies an integrated effort including elements of reconnaissance, electronic countermeasures (jamming), physical attack (destruction), and deception. Each of these elements helps disrupt effective enemy command and control at a critical decision point in battle. The Soviets continue to pursue REC efforts at strategic, operational, and tactical levels based on the advantage REC will give smaller Soviet combat forces. The effective employment of REC as a force multiplier becomes increasingly important to the Soviets as they restructure forces at all levels because of treaty arrangements.

Soviet efforts to collect information on US and NATO strategic command and control continue unabated. Signals intelligence collection against Western strategic command and control emissions gives the Soviets critical intelligence and warning information. It also supports strategic countermeasures' efforts. Soviet communica-

tions intercept and direction-finding sites provide a vast intelligence network spread across the USSR/Eastern Europe and in Soviet-aligned Third World nations around the globe.

Radars

Over the past decade, the Soviets have improved their air defense radars. New phased-array radars can detect and track multiple air targets better than their predecessors. Some new early warning radars are three-dimensional, eliminating the need for separate height-finder radars. Finally, the Soviets are working to close low-altitude radar gaps along their periphery, making undetected penetration by low-flying aircraft and cruise missiles more difficult.

Surface-to-Air Missiles (SAMs)

Soviet strategic SAMs (the SA-2, SA-3, SA-5, and SA-10) provide barrier, area, and point air defense of the Soviet Union. Since 1985, the number of strategic SAM sites and launchers has decreased as the USSR has retired older-generation systems. The SA-10 — in both fixed and mobile variations — is replacing older SA-2 and SA-3 SAM systems, improving Soviet air defense capabilities against low-altitude aircraft and cruise missile attacks. The SA-10's ability to engage several

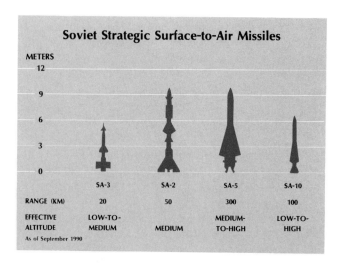

Soviet Strategic Surface-to-Air Missiles			
SA-3	SA-2	SA-5	SA-10
RANGE (KM) 20	50	300	100
EFFECTIVE ALTITUDE LOW-TO-MEDIUM	MEDIUM	MEDIUM-TO-HIGH	LOW-TO-HIGH

As of September 1990

targets simultaneously and its increased firepower (four missiles per launcher) have enhanced the Soviet Union's air defense capability. The SA-10 system currently constitutes approximately 25 percent of Soviet strategic SAM launchers.

Passive Defenses

The Soviet passive defense program is a significant

element of an integrated system of strategic defenses designed to moderate the effects of a nuclear attack. Passive defenses are designed to support wartime leadership continuity, economic mobilization, industrial base and essential work-force protection, and a credible reconstitution capability. The most important part of the Soviet passive defense program is an extensive, redundant set of hardened command posts and communications facilities for all key echelons of the military, party, and government apparatus.

For the past 40 years the Soviets have had a comprehensive program designed to ensure leadership continuity during a nuclear conflict. This effort has involved the construction of urban and exurban deep-underground facilities, near-surface bunkers, and secret subway evacuation lines for party, state, and military leadership elements at all levels. Although some of these facilities are already hundreds of meters deep and can hold thousands of people, the Soviets continue to upgrade, improve, and deepen them. The extensive preparations the Soviets have made for leadership protection and wartime management are designed to give their leaders the potential to operate effectively in a nuclear war environment. These leaders also have available redundant communications, and an array of ground-mobile, trainborne, and airborne command platforms.

Even Alexei Arbatov, a prominent civilian critic of many aspects of Soviet defense policy, including strategic defenses, has suggested that resources saved from other military programs could go to "raising the survivability, efficiency, and quality of our underground and airborne command and communications systems."

Prospects

The Soviets probably will continue to rely on both strategic offensive and defensive capabilities to limit damage to the homeland during nuclear war. Prominent Soviet civilian defense specialists have openly challenged the utility of strategic defenses in what appears to be an ongoing debate among Soviet officials. But, the vast level of resources that Moscow continues to expend on strategic defense programs in the face of an economic crisis shows a continuing commitment to reducing deficiencies in their defenses and a willingness to sacrifice in order to meet their wartime objectives. Their investment in strategic defenses, nearly equal to that of their offensive nuclear programs, thus is likely to remain near current levels.

Improvements can be cited in numerous areas. The Soviets will continue to upgrade their extensive air defense system through upgrades to early warning de-

tection, tracking, command and control, and intercept capabilities, especially against low-altitude aircraft. Ongoing enhancements will enable the USSR to engage targets farther outside national borders. Current modernization of the Soviet ABM system will be completed, and R&D in ABM technologies will continue. Improvements to radars and interceptors are expected which will enhance Soviet capabilities to intercept and destroy ballistic missiles. Finally, already extensive leadership and strategic materiel protection will be augmented with the construction of additional deep-underground facilities and near-surface bunkers.

SPACE FORCES

Introduction

The Soviets continue to improve their military space capabilities. Enhancements encompass both their orbital assets and their ground-based space support facilities. Although the USSR appears to be restructuring some of its operating principles regarding space, these efforts have not detracted from space-based support to military missions. The influence of *glasnost* on the Soviet space program has been significant, but public announcements regarding space programs focus primarily on commercial space promotion and budgetary justification of the civil space programs. Admissions of Soviet military use of space remain infrequent, and the economy measures reported by Soviet space program managers appear to be designed largely to avoid calls for further economic constraints. Despite restructuring in other military forces, the objectives of the Soviet military space program have not changed. Soviet military space strategy still requires sufficient capability to provide effective space-based support to Soviet terrestrial military forces and the capability to deny the use of space to other states.

Missions and Operations

The Soviet space program continues to be predominantly military in character, with most satellites dedicated either to exclusive military missions (such as reconnaissance and targeting) or to civil/military applications (such as communications and meteorology).

The most obvious change in Soviet space activity in 1989 was a dramatic decrease in space launches from an average of over 90 space launches a year from 1980 to 1988 to only 74 in 1989. A lower rate of launches thus far has continued during 1990, though military space capabilities remain steadfast. Over the years, the Soviets have steadily increased the number of operational satellites they maintain in orbit to over 160.

TASS/SOVFOTO

The *Buran* space shuttle is shown here carried on the An-225. The initial launch, flight, and return of *Buran,* conducted unmanned and entirely under automatic control on November 15, 1988, was an impressive technical achievement. The future employment of such orbital craft will further enhance Soviet space capabilites.

Soviet satellites are becoming more sophisticated and long-lived. This increased operational efficiency is the mark of a more mature military space program that can reduce redundancy while accomplishing its missions and retain the surge launch and reconstitution capabilities that are essential for military operations in crisis or conflict.

Space-Based Military Support

Recently, Soviet defense officials have testified to the importance they attribute to military space systems supporting terrestrial forces, calling them a force multiplier. An extensive array of spacecraft supports the Soviet armed forces and military and political leadership. Soviet satellite systems conduct a variety of missions: imagery, electronic, and radar reconnaissance; launch detection and attack warning; ocean surveillance and targeting; command, control, and communications; navigational and meteorological support; and military research and development. An extensive ground infrastructure supports the system. Despite the drop in launches in 1989, improvement, maintenance, or refurbishment of this infrastructure has remained active, indicating that Soviet military space capabilities likely will continue to improve in the future.

Antisatellite (ASAT) Systems

The Soviet military and political leadership is fully aware of the value of military space systems. The Soviets have, therefore, developed the capability to disrupt and destroy the military space systems of potential enemies. The USSR has a dedicated ASAT system which probably became operational in 1971. In August 1983 Moscow announced a unilateral moratorium on the launching of ASAT weapons. However, the Soviets routinely conduct tests of ASAT elements and procedures on the ground, and they use the associated booster, the SL-11, to launch ELINT Ocean Reconnaissance Satellites (EORSATs). The booster also is used to launch Radar Ocean Reconnaissance Satellites (RORSATs), although the last RORSAT launch was in 1988. The coorbital interceptor remains in readiness at its launch site at the Tyuratam cosmodrome, where two launch pads and storage space for many interceptors and launch vehicles are available, but has not been launched since 1982.

The Soviets maintain a significant ASAT capability against low-earth-orbit and medium-earth-orbit satellites, but capabilities against high-altitude ones are limited. Future ASAT developments could include new directed-energy weapons or direct-ascent nonnuclear interceptors.

The Soviets have additional potential ASAT capabilities: exoatmospheric ABM missiles, located around Moscow and at the Sary Shagan test range, that could be used against satellites in near-earth orbit; at least one

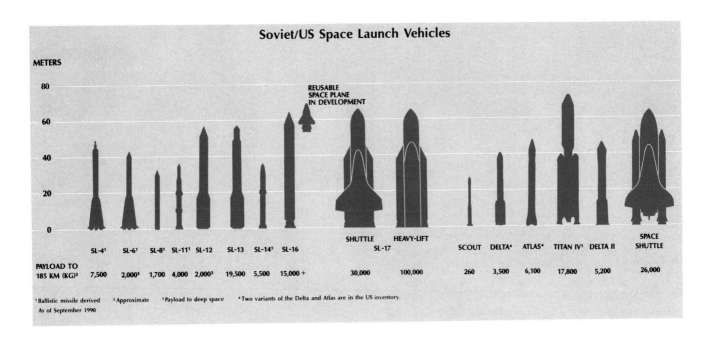

Soviet/US Space Launch Vehicles

METERS

PAYLOAD TO 185 KM (KG)[2]	SL-4[1]	SL-6[1]	SL-8[1]	SL-11[1]	SL-12	SL-13	SL-14[1]	SL-16	SHUTTLE SL-17	HEAVY-LIFT	SCOUT	DELTA[4]	ATLAS[4]	TITAN IV[1]	DELTA II	SPACE SHUTTLE
	7,500	2,000[3]	1,700	4,000	2,000[3]	19,500	5,500	15,000+	30,000	100,000	260	3,500	6,100	17,800	5,200	26,000

[1] Ballistic missile derived   [2] Approximate   [3] Payload to deep space   [4] Two variants of the Delta and Atlas are in the US inventory.
As of September 1990

ground-based laser, also at Sary Shagan, that may have sufficient power to damage some unprotected satellites in near-earth orbits; and electronic warfare assets that probably would be used against satellites at all altitudes. Research and development of technologies applicable to more advanced ASAT systems continue at a steady pace. Areas of investigation that appear to hold promise include high energy laser, particle beam, radio frequency, and kinetic energy technologies.

Manned Operations

After a four-month manning hiatus in mid-1989, the *Mir* space station complex was remanned and reactivated in early September. The Soviets vastly enhanced *Mir*'s capabilities for military and scientific research by launching the 20-ton *Kvant*-2 module in late November. As part of its equipment, *Kvant*-2 carries an external gimballed platform outfitted with a variety of sensors. While the Soviets report that these sensors are for earth-resource studies only, military applications also are highly likely. Cosmonaut military activity is another aspect of the Soviet space program which *glasnost* has yet to illuminate. *Kvant*-2 has a larger hatch for egress into space. It also delivered the Soviet version of a manned maneuvering unit to *Mir*.

Kristall, the materials technology module, was added to the *Mir* complex in June 1990 to facilitate the production of various materials under microgravity conditions.

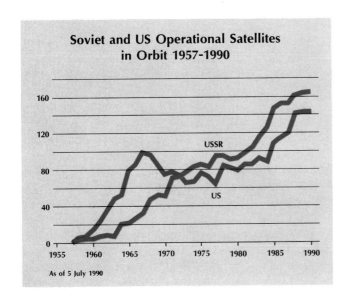

Soviet and US Operational Satellites in Orbit 1957-1990

As of 5 July 1990

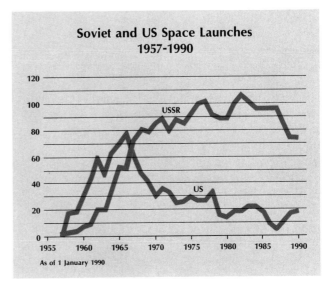

Soviet and US Space Launches 1957-1990

As of 1 January 1990

The *Vostok* space capsule continues as a work horse of the Soviet space program. This spacecraft, the same type used to launch Cosmonaut Yuri Gagarin in 1961, continues to be used today for a variety of military and civilian missions.

Such materials have civil applications, but the Soviet military-industrial complex also likely will be a prime user. *Kristall* also has a universal docking port that the Soviet space shuttle orbiter reportedly will use during its scheduled mission to *Mir* in 1991.

Four years after its launch, *Mir* is beginning to realize its potential as a military and scientific research platform with the addition of these two modules. It is still not clear whether it will profitably support civilian space ventures.

Space Launch Systems

Perhaps the strongest facets of the Soviet space program are its versatile and reliable inventory of space launch vehicles (SLVs) and its space launch and support facilities. Using these systems, the USSR can launch satellites very rapidly into a variety of orbits, a distinct operational military advantage in any crisis. Two newer systems, the SL-16 *(Zenit)* medium-lift SLV and the SL-17 *(Energiya)* heavy-lift SLV, significantly enhance Soviet launch capabilities. The Soviets announced in late 1989 that they would eventually replace the SL-4; the SL-16 may be the planned follow-on. A possible payload for the SL-16 might be a space plane. Some Soviet officials have stated that they used orbital and suborbital flights by an existing subscale version of a space plane to test their space shuttle, while others have said that the plane was an analogue to a space fighter. There are additional suggestions of a separate space plane program, including claims that such a system

might be launched off the new large Soviet transport, the An-225.

The USSR has also reported that its program for launching the SL-17 and the space shuttle orbiter will be "stretched out," for budgetary reasons. While cost may be a factor, it is likely that the primary missions for these systems are scheduled for the mid-1990s. Then the Soviets may begin to launch and assemble a new, very large space station composed of 100-ton, SL-17-launched modules. The shuttle orbiter will be most useful in support of this manned complex, although it also will be able to deploy and repair satellites, and to help with military research and development. Even with these new systems coming on-line, the Soviets continue to produce and launch their other SLVs at an impressive rate.

Prospects

While the Soviets have publicly described a new doctrine of "defense sufficiency" and have initiated large reductions in their conventional forces, they continue to maintain an impressive momentum of strategic nuclear arms modernization. Despite an ongoing crisis in the national economy, the Soviet leadership will continue to support strategic arms development since they believe that strategic nuclear forces present the primary external military threat to the Soviet Union, and define Soviet status as a superpower. The present trend toward a better mix of highly responsive silo-based ICBMs with more survivable mobile weapon systems almost certainly will continue into the 1990s. Strategic nuclear weapons based on mobile platforms will play a greater role than in the past in Soviet operational planning. Improvements in command and control, coupled with more capable ballistic and cruise missiles, will also enable the Soviets to field a more efficient nuclear force.

Along with strategic nuclear offensive modernization, the Soviets will continue their long-standing emphasis on strategic defense. They will finish the current upgrades to the ABM system around Moscow and continue R&D in ABM technologies. Modernization of air defenses also will continue. Although the Soviets have made a considerable investment in the leadership protection program, expansion and improvement of facilities probably will take place. Strategic defense, both active and passive, is viewed by the Soviets as an essential component of a warfighting strategy.

With the restructuring of their strategic nuclear forces to meet START-mandated reductions, the importance of space in maintaining control of and supporting these forces looms larger for the Soviet Union and the United

States. The Soviets recognize the vital importance to both superpowers of command and control of strategic nuclear forces. They also recognize that space systems provide essential support to a variety of military missions. Therefore, they will maintain their capability to conduct ASAT operations, modernize their satellites, and upgrade their ground-based space-related infrastructure. Soviet strategists believe that the military use of space is becoming more significant and want to be positioned to exploit space militarily.

THE STRATEGIC BALANCE

Background

The consequences of continued Soviet investment in strategic nuclear forces must be carefully weighed against US strategic forces as they relate to each nation's strategy and doctrine and the potential effects of arms control agreements. US security rests on the continued credibility of its nuclear forces as a deterrent to the Soviet Union.

An effective strategic deterrent rests on several factors. First, US strategic nuclear forces must possess qualities which render them effective, flexible, survivable, and enduring. Second, the United States must convince the Soviet leadership of its resolve to employ nuclear forces if necessary in response to attack. Third, the United States must accurately assess the evolving strategic balance and prevent the rise of major asymmetries as the Soviet Union continues to modernize its forces. Any failure of deterrence would probably arise from a conclusion by the Soviet leadership that trends in the strategic balance or Western resolve had increased the probability that the Soviet Union could attain its wartime objectives at an acceptable level of risk. Therefore, both US and Soviet defense experts go to great lengths to assess the strategic balance to ensure that gaps in force structure or policy do not appear.

No single measure exists for assessing a nation's military power or for evaluating the strategic balance between nations. Common assessments of strategic balance involve static measures of relative Soviet and US strategic nuclear force capabilities such as the number of strategic nuclear delivery vehicles (launchers) and associated warheads. These measures provide data for assessing the relative vulnerability of US strategic forces to a Soviet first strike and thereby allow some insight into the viability of the US deterrent.

Although quantitative measures provide a useful starting point for an assessment of the strategic balance and indeed form the basis for most arms control agreements,

US and Soviet defense experts would agree that looking at total numbers of weapons is insufficient to determine actual military capabilities. Each component of Soviet and US strategic forces, bombers, ICBMs, and SLBMs, has unique characteristics with respect to accuracy, responsiveness, survivability, and endurance. For example, the disparity between US and Soviet bomber forces is misleading since US strategic bombers must fly against highly developed air defenses, while Soviet bombers face only minimal defenses on the US side. Thus, differences of opinion regarding the strategic balance usually do not concern the number of weapons in each arsenal but rather the interpretation of the differences between the two and the importance of relative strengths and weaknesses in each.

Static Measures

Although the Soviet Union possesses significantly greater numbers of strategic nuclear delivery systems — launchers — than does the United States, a rough parity exists between the US and the Soviet Union with regard to the number of strategic offensive weapons. Under the START Treaty, both sides will be constrained to a ceiling of 6,000 accountable weapons and 4,900 ballistic missile reentry vehicles (RVs), even though there will be flexibility regarding force structure within that ceiling. Moreover, the "discounting" of bomber weapons in START will permit each side to deploy substantially more strategic weapons than the 6,000 limit.

Dynamic Assessment

Despite the expected reductions in Soviet force levels, based on the START agreement, an assessment of qualitative factors reveals important asymmetries between the United States and the Soviet Union. Qualitative factors, defined as those factors which influence the specific characteristics of each nation's arsenal, include: strategic doctrine, particularly with respect to the initiation of nuclear weapons' use; operational planning; operational characteristics of target bases; targeting policies; and trends in modernization. Doctrine, which underpins strategy and determines the composition of each nation's strategic force, is particularly important, since the asymmetries which exist between US and Soviet strategic forces stem in large part from divergences in doctrine.

Doctrine

Historically, pronounced differences have existed between the United States and the Soviet Union concerning their military doctrines and rationales supporting the existence and governing the use of nuclear weapons. The

US, through the policies of deterrence, strategic stability, and flexible response, has consistently maintained that a nuclear war cannot be won and should never be fought. As a result, three fundamental objectives underpin US strategic nuclear policy:

- Maintain effective deterrence. An effective strategic deterrent ensures that there are no circumstances that could arise that would lead the Soviet leadership to conclude that it could successfully launch an attack against the United States or its allies.
- Foster strategic stability. Strategic stability is a condition whereby neither the United States nor the Soviet Union is pressured to use nuclear weapons preemptively.
- Maintain the capability, if deterrence fails, to respond flexibly to a Soviet first strike. US leaders and military planners believe that a range of choices — with respect to both the timing and scale of a nuclear exchange with the Soviet Union — allows US decisionmakers to respond credibly to various Soviet attack scenarios, and thereby attempt to reestablish deterrence at the lowest level of violence.

Soviet views, objectives, and policies concerning the use of strategic nuclear weapons stand in sharp contrast to those of the United States. While the Soviet leadership publicly rejects its previous statements that a nuclear war could be fought and won by the Soviet Union, corresponding changes in Soviet force posture or adjustments in some key modernization efforts have yet to emerge. Similarly, even though Soviet leaders believe that a nuclear war would be highly destructive, militarily undesirable, and should be avoided if possible,

they nevertheless believe that should nuclear war occur it would be possible to enhance Soviet chances of emerging in a better condition than its enemies following a nuclear conflict and enable the leadership to retain political control. This belief has led the Soviet leadership to develop strategic offensive forces capable of seizing the strategic initiative through pre-emptive missile attack in the presence of clear evidence that the other side was about to launch a nuclear attack. To limit damage, the Soviet Union has also consistently pursued the development of advanced strategic defenses through a vast, interlocking, and redundant system of active and passive defenses. These objectives have, more than any other factor, governed the allocation of scarce resources in favor of robust strategic capabilities.

Composition of Forces

Differences in the composition of US and Soviet strategic nuclear forces are a direct reflection of differences between US and Soviet nuclear doctrine. The United States has developed a strategic triad of ICBMs, SLBMS, and bombers, providing flexibility and survivability which hedge against unforeseen developments that might threaten US retaliatory capabilities. Specifically, each leg of the Triad has unique capabilities that complement those of the others. Silo-based ICBMs provide great promptness and accuracy. SLBMs provide survivability, flexibility, and endurance. Bombers provide alert launch survivability, recallability, and employment flexibility. The different basing modes and means of penetration in the Triad contribute importantly to an aggressor's uncertainty about his ability to attack pre-emptively or to defend against a US retaliatory

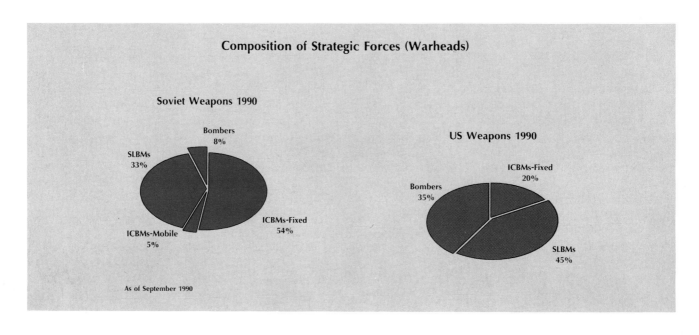

Composition of Strategic Forces (Warheads)

Soviet Weapons 1990

Bombers 8%
SLBMs 33%
ICBMs-Mobile 5%
ICBMs-Fixed 54%

As of September 1990

US Weapons 1990

ICBMs-Fixed 20%
Bombers 35%
SLBMs 45%

Strategic Offensive Forces
(As of July 1990)

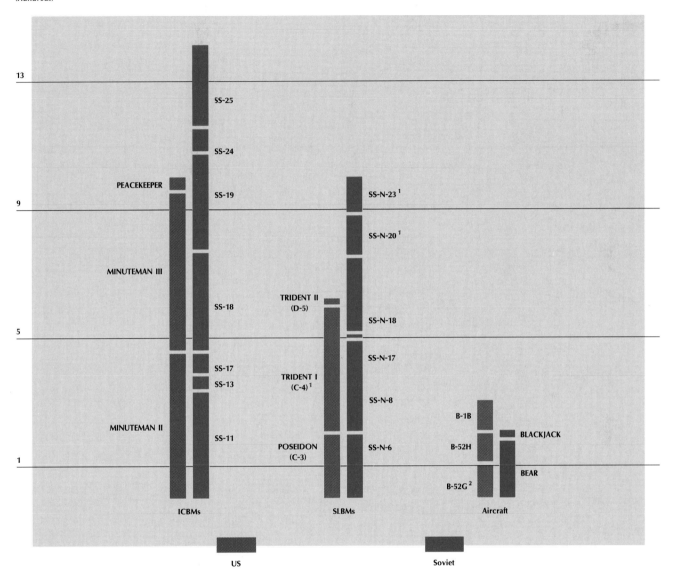

Total
(Hundreds)

13

9

5

1

PEACEKEEPER

MINUTEMAN III

MINUTEMAN II

SS-25
SS-24
SS-19
SS-18
SS-17
SS-13
SS-11

ICBMs

TRIDENT II
(D-5)

TRIDENT I
(C-4)[1]

POSEIDON
(C-3)

SLBMs

SS-N-23[1]
SS-N-20[1]
SS-N-18
SS-N-17
SS-N-8
SS-N-6

B-1B
B-52H
B-52G[2]

BLACKJACK
BEAR

Aircraft

US

Soviet

[1] Includes SLBMs potentially carried on Trident, Typhoon, and Delta-IV submarines on sea trials.

[2] The B-52G bombers include aircraft that are assigned conventional missions.

attack. They also are intended to provide the US President with confidence in his ability to retain options for retaliation, thus reducing any unwarranted pressures for nuclear escalation in a crisis.

The Soviet Union has, on the other hand, developed a nuclear force that includes heavy ICBMs with first-strike capabilities, prompt hard-target-kill capability, a large number of RVs, and high-yield warheads.

These charts bear out these assertions. For instance,

approximately 80 percent of US strategic nuclear weapons are located in the bomber and submarine legs — increasing the flexibility and survivability of US strategic forces. In contrast, almost two-thirds of Soviet nuclear warheads are on ICBMs. Thus, while the US ICBM leg has the capability to deter a Soviet strike, it does not provide the same destructive capacity, destabilizing characteristics, or first-strike capabilities as does its Soviet counterpart.

Trends in Soviet modernization will, however, result

The Ohio-class ballistic missile submarine is now armed with the new Trident II (D-5) missile. The Trident II delivers a larger payload than current SLBMs, with significantly improved accuracy, at a nominal range of 7,400 km. Nine of these boats are operational, and eight others are in various stages of construction.

in a strategic force which is more balanced among ICBMs, bombers, and SLBMs. At the same time, these forces will be more lethal, more survivable and, under the START agreement, smaller. The Soviet drive towards a better-balanced strategic force structure with highly survivable and capable components theoretically puts the Soviet leadership in a position to consider a move away from its current first-strike posture to one which allows for flexible response and limited nuclear options.

Currently, the US strategic modernization program is increasing the capability and survivability of US offensive forces. The deployment of a limited, 50-missile Peacekeeper force reduces the Soviet advantage in prompt hard-target-kill capability, although the Soviet lead in ICBMs continues. US Ohio-class SSBNs, armed with the Trident D-5 missile since March 1990; B-1B bombers; and ALCMs — possessing greater survivability, accuracy, and effectiveness than older systems — enable the US to sustain advantages in submarines and bombers, offsetting Soviet advantages in ICBMs.

Longer-term projections of the balance depend, in part, on resolution of the uncertainties which currently surround the pace and overall level of the US strategic modernization program. For example, planned US mobile ICBMs provide increased survivability and stability

and can hold hardened targets at risk, but the US has not yet deployed them. The penetration capability and operational flexibility of the B-2 bomber and advanced cruise missile (ACM) will significantly stress Soviet air defenses and maintain the effectiveness of US air-breathing forces, further enhancing deterrence.

Modernization and Production Trends

Since the mid-1960s, the Soviets have engaged in a brisk program of strategic modernization while US spending on strategic forces for the most part stayed flat and even declined at times. Today, the Soviet strategic forces which were modernized in the late 1970s and early 1980s remain a formidable force. In 1989, the Soviet Union deployed over 100 new ICBMs, two new SSBNs, and several Bear H and Blackjack bombers as compared to the United States which added only one SSBN, and no new ICBMs, or bombers to its operational forces.

While the current US strategic modernization program is increasing the capability and survivability of US forces, the differentials in the pace of modernization and the rate of production have, in fact, resulted in notable asymmetries. To begin with, substantial portions of US strategic forces are rapidly approaching the end of their useful service lives. In addition, Soviet force improvements increasingly reduce the capability of some aging US forces. For example, Soviet strategic defenses — which have received funding priority nearly equal to strategic offensive programs since the 1960s — threaten US bomber forces, particularly the B-52. As a penetrator, the B-52 is no longer optimally suited to challenge directly the increasingly sophisticated Soviet air defense network; in particular, its large radar cross section (RCS) makes it susceptible to enemy detection. Furthermore, its slow-reaction take-off and its insufficient hardening against nuclear effects do not provide a desirable margin of safety to hedge against pre-emptive SLBM attacks on US bomber bases.

Strategic Defenses

Traditionally, the Soviet Union has pursued development of both active and passive strategic defenses in order to limit damage to the Soviet Union in the event of a war. The United States, on the other hand, has followed a policy of offensive deterrence based on the rationale that neither the United States nor the Soviet Union would launch a nuclear first strike or engage in other highly provocative actions if both sides were vulnerable to nuclear retaliation. But continued Soviet interest in strategic defenses and promising new technologies have contributed to a reassessment of traditional US assumptions.

The Soviet Union deploys the world's only ABM system and the world's most extensive air defense system. As a result of strategic air defenses, the Soviet Union

Currently, the US strategic modernization program is increasing the capability and survivability of US offensive forces. The deployment of a limited, 50-missile Peacekeeper force reduces the Soviet advantage in hard-target-kill capability, although the Soviet lead in ICBMs continues. Here, Peacekeeper reentry vehicles pass through the atmosphere at the conclusion of a test flight.

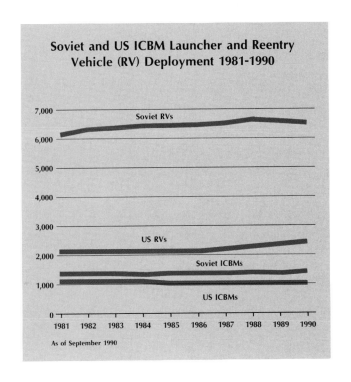

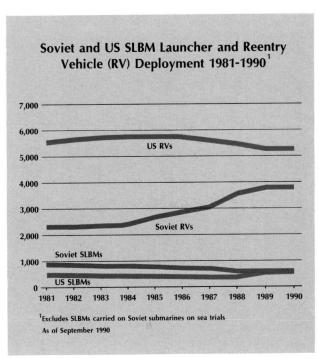

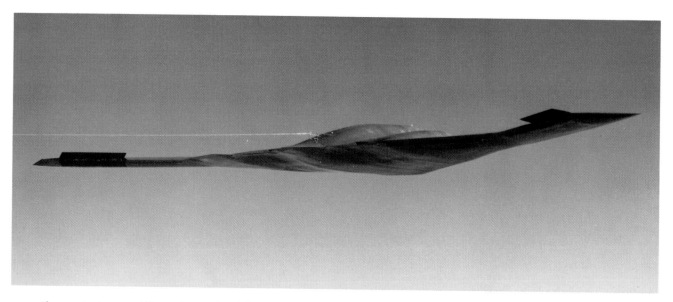

The penetration capability and operational flexibility of the B-2 bomber and advanced cruise missile (ACM) will significantly stress Soviet air defenses and maintain the effectiveness of US air-breathing forces, further enhancing deterrence.

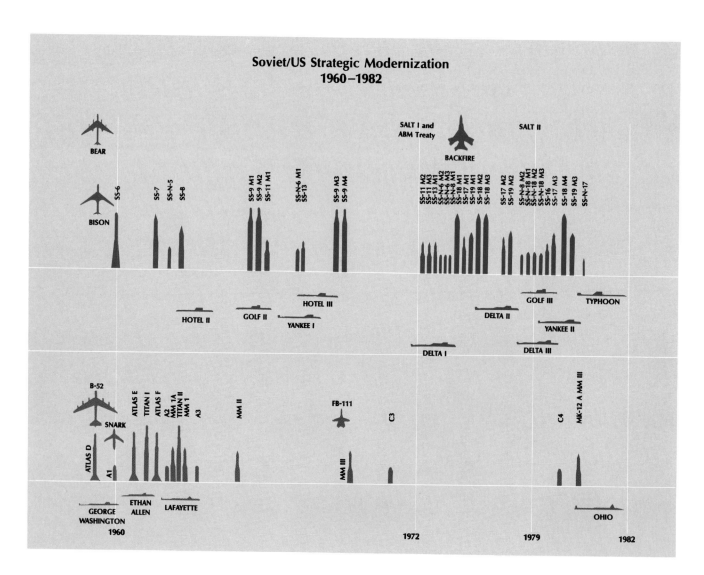

Soviet/US Strategic Modernization
1960–1982

has the capability to decrease the extent of wartime damage to the Soviet Union. Moreover, Soviet strategic defenses are capable of degrading the effectiveness of US offensive forces. For example, the ability of US bomber forces — which comprise more than one-third of US strategic offensive forces — to penetrate Soviet airspace is challenged by continuing improvements in Soviet air defenses. US air defenses, by comparison, are less extensive and are dedicated to providing warning and attack assessment — in short, we would probably be able to detect Soviet bombers coming but would be limited in our ability to stop them from completing their attacks.

Despite these obvious asymmetries, the Soviet Union continues to modernize its strategic air defenses. Indeed, current funding for these programs continues to show support for a long-term commitment to strategic defense — even as those efforts are somewhat moderated by a deepening economic crisis and rising political pressures. For example:

- The Soviet Union continues to upgrade its ABM system around Moscow, which provides dual-layered coverage through endo- and exoatmospheric interceptors. Although this system would not provide significant protection against a US retaliatory strike, it could protect against limited strikes initiated by other countries. Furthermore, the Moscow ABM system provides the Soviets with valuable experience operating ballistic missile defenses.
- Soviet SAMs provide barrier, area, and point air defense of the Soviet Union. The Soviet Union continues to deploy SA-10s, which have the ability to engage several targets simultaneously, dramatically enhancing the Soviet Union's air defense capabilities. The United States, on the other hand, has not fielded strategic defenses of this quantity or quality. Moreover, Soviet deployment of SA-10s has continued at a level which allows the Soviet Union to increase its active inventory each month at a rate greater than the United States can increase its global inventory of Patriot air defenses in an entire year.

Overall, therefore, continued Soviet commitment to upgrading their strategic defenses with an array of ABMs, SAMs, fourth-generation fighter-interceptors, computer-assisted command and control systems, and modern three-dimensional radars stands in sharp contrast to the comparatively limited US strategic defenses.

The Soviet Union also places great emphasis on passive defenses to protect its key assets from US retaliation. For example, the Soviet Union continues to increase the survivability of its ICBMs by hardening missile silos. In addition, the Soviet Union has built deep-underground bunkers to protect key political, mili-

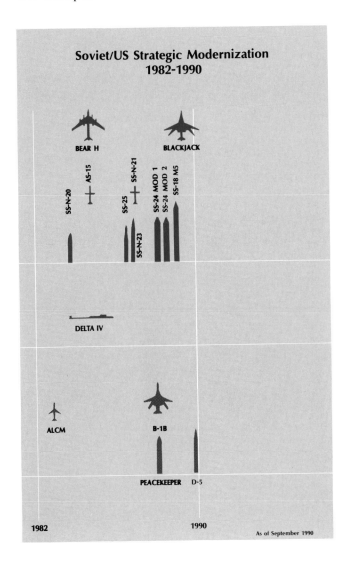

**Soviet/US Strategic Modernization
1982-1990**

BEAR H   BLACKJACK

SS-N-20   AS-15   SS-25   SS-N-21   SS-N-23   SS-24 MOD 1   SS-24 MOD 2   SS-18 M5

DELTA IV

ALCM   B-1B

PEACEKEEPER   D-5

1982   1990

As of September 1990

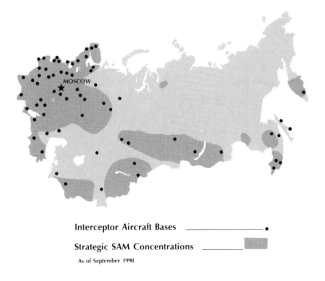

Soviet Territorial Air Defense

MOSCOW

Interceptor Aircraft Bases _____ •

Strategic SAM Concentrations _____ ▓

As of September 1990

The Soviet Union has begun deployment of newly modernized surface-to-air missiles — SA-10s — which have the ability to engage several targets simultaneously, with increased firepower. Soviet SAMs provide barrier, area, and point air defense.

tary, and industry personnel in the event of a nuclear exchange. The US has not developed comparable passive defenses due to the prevailing rationale that neither side would launch a first strike if both sides were vulnerable to nuclear retaliation.

Decades of continued Soviet progress in upgrading its strategic defenses, combined with their ongoing modernization of Soviet strategic offenses, threatens to reduce significantly the stability of offensive deterrence. Several factors have caused the US, through the Strategic Defense Initiative, to examine the feasibility of advanced defenses against ballistic missiles. These include the asymmetry in strategic defenses, the US desire to reduce reliance on the threat of offensive retaliation to ensure deterrence, and the advent of promising defensive technologies.

In summary, important asymmetries exist in the balance between US and Soviet strategic forces. While strategic offensive weapons will be constrained to the same levels by START, qualitative differences in strategic offensive weapon systems and robust Soviet strategic defenses favor the Soviet Union. These asymmetries may be attributed to long-standing differences in doctrine and trends in modernization efforts.

START Objectives and Outcomes

The Soviets have a keen interest in concluding a START agreement, despite resistance to certain compromises. The political and economic benefits and proposed follow-on reduction and stability talks are also important for long-term Soviet interests. The fundamental motivations for the Soviets to engage in strategic

arms reduction remain unchanged since START negotiations began: to maintain a favorable strategic balance, to avoid open-ended spending on strategic programs, and to enhance the international position of the USSR.

The United States has pursued four main objectives in negotiating the START Treaty.

- To encourage the Soviet Union to decrease its reliance on destabilizing systems, particularly heavy ICBMs;
- To encourage the expansion of stabilizing systems, particularly "slow flyers" — i.e., bombers, rather than ballistic missiles;
- To maintain flexibility for the post-START force; and
- To enhance deterrence and encourage strategic stability at lower levels of forces.

The US has largely succeeded in achieving these goals.

While START will be the first arms control agreement to achieve a real reduction in strategic forces, the Treaty does not restrict the rapidly evolving technologies which have resulted in the deployment of increasingly capable Soviet strategic offensive and defensive weapon systems. As a result, even as Soviet weapons are reduced, overall Soviet capabilities may remain largely unchanged and could even increase over time.

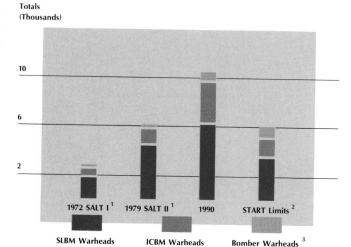

Changes in Soviet Strategic Offensive Warheads (1972-1990)

[1] Neither SALT I nor SALT II placed limits on ballistic missile warheads. Data reflect Soviet ballistic missile warheads on these dates.

[2] The United States and Soviet Union have agreed to a sublimit ceiling of 4,900 on the aggregate number of ICBM plus SLBM warheads. The United States has proposed a 3,000-3,300 limit on ICBM warheads.

[3] Nominal loading

As of September 1990

The space shuttle Columbia lifts off launch pad 39B at Cape Canaveral on a Department of Defense mission.

For example, under the START Treaty, Soviet throwweight and Soviet heavy missiles will be reduced by about 50 percent. While real benefits accrue to the United States based on this reduction, strategic modernization will allow Soviet military planners potentially to replace some of the capability lost by these reductions with the effectiveness gained through increased accuracy of new systems.

Balance in Space

Recognizing the effectiveness and efficiency of space systems, both the United States and the Soviet Union have become dependent on space systems for support of military operations, whether in the theater or strategic arena. The United States has progressed to the point where many military support functions are provided primarily by space systems. The Soviets, on the other hand, have maintained terrestrial alternatives to space systems but are also developing space systems which are reliable and capable enough to perform these functions. In fact, statements by high-level Soviet officials suggest that the importance of space systems may increase with the reduction of Soviet terrestrial forces.

There are notable differences between US and Soviet military space programs. The United States has an integrated force structure, including highly capable, long-lived satellites, launch vehicles, launch facilities, and ground control elements to achieve "assured mission capability" — the ability to guarantee that critical missions can be accomplished, regardless of failure of individual system elements. In contrast, the Soviet space force structure utilizes satellites which are usually less capable and have shorter lifetimes. The Soviets, therefore, rely on more frequent launches, supported by robust production resources. Despite indications of a reduced peacetime launch rate, it appears that their infrastructure will continue to provide the Soviets with an advantage in space support responsiveness useful for wartime.

In addition to their space systems supporting terrestrial military operations, the Soviets possess the world's only operational ASAT weapon, as well as several other systems with ASAT capability. These systems provide the Soviets with the capability to hold US space systems in orbit at risk, with the option to degrade or destroy those systems in time of crisis or conflict.

VI

General Purpose Forces
and the US-Soviet Balance

Modifications to Soviet military doctrine and unilateral force reductions notwithstanding, improvements in weapon systems continue to enhance capabilities. This new BMP-3 infantry fighting vehicle, of which some 700 are expected to be produced during 1990, was shown for the first time on parade in Moscow during May.

INTRODUCTION

The continuing implementation of announced force reductions, Moscow's tacit acceptance of the dissolution of the Warsaw Pact as a cohesive military alliance, and further anticipated changes in Soviet force structure in Europe and throughout the Soviet Union indicate a dramatic shift in Soviet military policy and perspective. This shift parallels historic changes in Soviet domestic economic plans and national priorities, as detailed in the initial chapters of this publication. Taken together, this comprehensive series of changes in almost every aspect of Soviet society has vastly complicated the difficult task of assessing the consequences of these events for Soviet military capabilities. The atmosphere of hope and expectation that has been sparked by the Kremlin's departure from its past orthodoxy has accentuated the importance of determining how the West should respond to best encourage Soviet development, while ensuring the security interests of the United States and its allies.

To provide a basis for this assessment, this chapter details the comprehensive force structure changes that are under way in the Soviet military. The final section examines the implications of these changes for the military balance in the regions where Soviet forces operate.

Theater Strategy: Strategic Defense Concepts

The Soviets envision a strategic defense as a theater-level operation to drive back an attacking enemy, avoid nuclear escalation and geographic spread of war, obtain a negotiated termination of the conflict, and, if that is not possible, create conditions for a possible deep offensive to defeat the enemy. The Soviets continue a historic emphasis on the critical need to gain and maintain the initiative. Their operations could include defensive actions combined with counterattacks and counterstrikes conducted by highly maneuverable combined-arms forces with supporting artillery, missiles, and air strikes.

Theater Warfighting Capabilities

Soviet planners were critically dependent on non-Soviet Warsaw Pact (NSWP) forces to participate in multi-front operations in a coordinated theater strategic operation against NATO. Given the sweeping changes in Eastern Europe, the Soviets can no longer depend on NSWP forces for theater offensive operations nor can they rule out the active resistance of East European militaries. This would mean that up to one-half of the first echelon forces in the Western Theater of Military Operations might not be available for offensive operations against NATO. While the theoretical capability for a Pact theater strategic operation will remain until a Conventional Armed Forces in Europe (CFE) agree-

ment is implemented, political realities preclude such an operation.

Changes in Command Structure

Notwithstanding the dramatic political changes that are transforming the Warsaw Pact, the Soviet General Staff likely still sees the necessity to structure its forces to confront enemy coalitions in widely separated theaters of military operations (TVDs) in Europe, the Far East, and Southwest Asia. Permanent peacetime regional high commands were formed to act as extensions of the General Staff. These commands centralized control over the ground, tactical air, air defense, and general purpose naval forces supporting operations in each of the TVDs on the Soviet periphery. The existence of these strategic command and control bodies in peacetime is intended to ease the transition of Soviet and Warsaw Pact command structures and forces to a war footing as well as enhance the Soviet military command, control, and communication (C^3) system's potential to cope with the demands of a multitheater war.

The withdrawal of Soviet forces from Eastern Europe may eventually lead to a theater command structure based largely on facilities located solely within the Soviet Union itself — a radical departure from the existing system. As Soviet forces withdraw, the extent to which the existing infrastructure of bunkered command posts (CPs) and hardened communications facilities in Eastern Europe will stay intact is unclear. Many of the facilities and much of the infrastructure used by Soviet forces in Eastern Europe are being destroyed during the withdrawal period. The Soviets probably will seek to negotiate bilateral agreements with their allies to ensure that key facilities remain operational, possibly by being maintained in a caretaker status. The restoration of bilateral military cooperation would depend primarily on political decisions, but the complete destruction of the base infrastructure would significantly complicate any renewal of military capabilities.

Fronts, consisting of several tank and combined-arms armies and organic air forces that are roughly equivalent to NATO army groups, would comprise the bulk of the forces that each high command would control in wartime. High commands can also control assets of a

Fleet and Air Armies of the Supreme Command.

To direct complex theater-strategic operations effectively, the Soviets and their allies established a comprehensive and redundant network of fixed and mobile CPs and supporting communications along the periphery of the Soviet Union, in Eastern Europe, and in Mongolia. The foundation of this system is an extensive network of bunkered CPs and communications facilities to accommodate high command staffs and their subordinates in wartime. To enhance network survivability, major CPs are equipped with buried antennas, separate hardened radio transmitters, and retractable communications antennas. In addition, theater-wide fixed communications networks incorporating a variety of redundant communication means link the bunkered CPs with General Staff facilities and those in adjacent theaters. Despite the force reductions and withdrawals now in progress, the theater C^3 infrastructure in the Soviet Union itself continues to expand.

To complement the fixed CP system, an array of field-mobile CPs and communications units for theater forces is deployed at all levels of command. At the higher levels of command, field-mobile CPs would be used primarily to supplement the system of large CP bunkers from

---

PERESTROIKA AND THE ARMED FORCES

Five years into Gorbachev's tenure, the Soviet military — previously a much respected and privileged organization — is an institution in turmoil. Some of the turmoil stems from adjusting to real changes in military doctrine, structure, and force levels. Some results from the military's uncertain role in a fast-changing political environment.

Changes affecting the political system have resulted in a substantial decline in the military's prestige; increasing pressure to end the draft; and a major change in the way military decisions are made, with a much broader array of participants, many of whom are hostile to military interests. Rising nationalism in some minority republics has led to republic demands that minority youth be allowed to serve in their home republics. These sentiments have been fueled by the use of Defense Ministry forces in regions of ethnic violence. These trends are having an increasingly negative effect on military morale and have been particularly demoralizing for the Soviet officer corps — the backbone of the armed forces.

Economic considerations are only one factor behind the current debate on manning and restructuring in the Soviet armed forces. Many of the proposals under debate would not substantially lower costs; one of them — the proposed shift to a volunteer military — would probably cost more than the large conscript army it would replace. Doctrinal developments dovetail with trends affecting military technology. They point toward a different kind of system than the large standing army Gorbachev inherited. For example, integrating more sophisticated equipment into the armed forces has increased the need for training and specialized skills. As the technological complexity of weaponry increases, the extensive use of conscripts in the armed forces impairs the full potential of high-technology weapons.

In addition, Gorbachev's political reforms are changing the nature of the policymaking system itself by bringing in new groups that are dubious about the strong commitment to military power of the previous leaders. For example, minority activists are hostile to the military in general and the draft in particular. Some regard the armed forces as a dramatic symbol of centralized Soviet power. Protests against the draft or against stationing Soviet forces on republic territory have become more popular as a means of expressing minority demands. The conscript army remains largely intact after nearly five years of perestroika, but there is increasing criticism from groups in the Supreme Soviet and reform groups in the military that call into question many of the assumptions underlying the use of minority soldiers. These reformers propose modifications of draft policy and replacing conscripts with a volunteer military.

Compared to the large-scale force reductions, withdrawals, and restructuring under way in the other branches of the Soviet armed forces, the Navy has emerged from Gorbachev's first round of defense cuts relatively unscathed. The reasons for this privileged status are many. First, the Soviet Navy's surface fleet is primarily a defensively oriented force whose structure is more compatible with Gorbachev's stated "defensive doctrine." Second, the Soviets believe that their Navy is inferior to combined Western navies, thus senior naval officers are able to make a strong case for continued fleet modernization. Finally, and most importantly, the Navy's SSBN force is becoming an increasingly important part of Soviet strategic nuclear forces.

Perestroika has also meant that the use of military power for foreign policy goals in the Third World has been significantly deemphasized. As a result, the Soviet Navy has diminished its out-of-area presence considerably. Excluding SSBN activity, worldwide Soviet Navy out-of-area presence has declined by approximately 20 percent from the peak pre-Gorbachev levels.

Reductions have also occurred in operating tempo — the ratio of days at sea to days available to go to sea. More emphasis is being placed on short in-area operations with intensive multiple training objectives, increased use of simulators and pierside training devices, and expanded combined air defense operations. As a result, the Soviet Navy's overall operating tempo has also declined by approximately 20 percent from 1985-levels.

ROLE OF MILITARY/MVD/KGB BORDER GUARDS IN INTERNAL CONTROL

Soviet law delegates the internal security responsibility to the security forces, rather than the armed forces. Moscow maintains two security troop formations — the Border Troops of the Committee for State Security (KGB) and the Internal Troops of the Ministry of Internal Affairs (MVD) — that are excluded from the control of the armed forces. The Border Troops are Moscow's eyes and ears along the Russian land and sea littorals, while the Internal Troops maintain the peace among the population.

Recent Soviet official statements on the missions of each service are:

Border Troops: "Those elements responsible for checking every transient — and apprehending those illegally crossing the border." Organizationally, the Border Guard elements observe the borders, patrol the adjacent Soviet border zones, and send appropriate formations in response to unusual situations.

Internal Troops: "Those elements designed to disperse those involved in mass disturbances, guard places of confinement and similar operations, protect properties of the State, and convey persons and property to prescribed destinations, in accordance with the law of the duties and rights of the Internal Troops of the MVD." The Soviet Government has officially stated that the use of Soviet armed forces in internal disputes was ill-considered, and indicated elements of the armed forces would not be used in contingencies within the Soviet Union. (The presence of military units in the Transcaucasus and Lithuania directly contradicts these statements.)

Recent engagements involving Border and/or Internal Troop elements reflect evolving roles for the two services. The period of unrest which occurred in the Transcaucasus this past January, given its proximity to the border, resulted in the involvement of Border Troop units. Although their exact role is not certain, it appeared that they were engaged in securing the borders following large demonstrations at border crossing points. In fact, the entire area of unrest may have been assigned to the control of the Border Troops. Ground and Internal Troop units relocated to the area may have been controlled by the Border Guard commander.

Historically, the insertion of Internal Troops into areas of civil unrest has been dictated by defense laws. A decision to deploy elements is always pursuant to a request for assistance by officials of the individual republics. The number and frequency of such requests has required continuing deployment of Ground Forces elements to support the Internal Troop units. Internal Troop officials admit to being stretched too thinly with the forces allotted, and have begun a program of expanding their structure. The question of the legality of the deployment of Internal Troop units, officially resubordinated from the Defense Ministry to the MVD early in 1989, was addressed in the recently enacted Law on MVD Internal Troops. The decision to deploy the forces can now be made also by decree of the Soviet President.

NOVOSTI/SOVFOTO

Troops of the Ministry of Internal Affairs, trained to suppress demonstrations and maintain order, stand shoulder-to-shoulder in Moscow in the midst of protests against the Soviet Communist Party.

NOVOSTI/SOVFOTO

which staffs would direct operations, and to replace damaged or destroyed CPs. At lower levels, command functions would be exercised from field-mobile CPs once force mobilization was completed. Small airborne battle staffs provide an additional layer of redundancy at each echelon, although they are inherently less capable than the larger ground-based CPs.

In addition to an extensive fixed communication network, the theater command system also relies on a variety of mobile communication means to include satellite, tropospheric scatter, high-frequency radio, line-of-sight radio relay, and cable communications systems. To support the control and forward movement of forces, mobile communications units would extend and, when necessary, reconstitute the fixed network. The KGB also operates separate, parallel communications at key echelons of command within Soviet theater forces.

GROUND FORCES

After a full year of force reductions, restructuring, reorganization, and modernization, the Soviets have reduced the number of active divisions from 214 to about 190. The number of mobilization divisions has increased from three to six. At the same time, the Soviets have continued their modernization program. This has included the production and introduction into the force of up to 1,700 late-model tanks, 6,500 armored infantry fighting vehicles, and 2,350 late-model self-propelled artillery and heavy mortars. In the maneuver divisions, air defense units at the regimental level have been expanded and upgraded with the new armored, self-propelled 2S6 and the highly capable SA-18 shoulder-launched missile (replacing the ZSU-23-4 and the SA-7 and SA-14). At the army and front level, the SA-11 and SA-12 surface-to-air missiles are replacing the aging SA-4.

As part of the new defensive doctrine, assault bridging equipment is being withdrawn from forward-deployed positions in the Warsaw Pact countries. After a full year of force reductions, restructuring, reorganization, and modernization, the Soviets have reduced the number of active divisions from 214 to about 190.

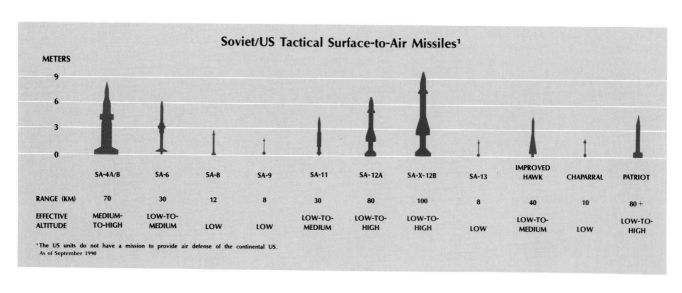

Soviet/US Tactical Surface-to-Air Missiles[1]

METERS	SA-4A/B	SA-6	SA-8	SA-9	SA-11	SA-12A	SA-X-12B	SA-13	IMPROVED HAWK	CHAPARRAL	PATRIOT
RANGE (KM)	70	30	12	8	30	80	100	8	40	10	80+
EFFECTIVE ALTITUDE	MEDIUM-TO-HIGH	LOW-TO-MEDIUM	LOW	LOW	LOW-TO-MEDIUM	LOW-TO-HIGH	LOW-TO-HIGH	LOW	LOW-TO-MEDIUM	LOW	LOW-TO-HIGH

[1] The US units do not have a mission to provide air defense of the continental US.
As of September 1990

The reorganization of divisions to the structure Gorbachev termed "clearly defensive" has taken place primarily in the Groups of Forces stationed in East European countries. The main feature of the program is to transform maneuver divisions away from an overtly offensive character by reducing the number of tanks in tank and motorized rifle divisions by 20 and 40 percent, respectively. This is being accomplished by converting one tank regiment in each to a motorized rifle regiment and by increasing the number of defensive systems such as antitank, air defense, and engineer obstacle equipment. What has not been widely publicized is the fact that the new structure is a well-balanced combat force featuring a significant increase of artillery systems, armored infantry fighting vehicles, and personnel.

Ground Forces Equipment

Modern main battle tanks (MBTs) — the T-72 and T-80 variants — continue to be produced and replace older tanks that are now being withdrawn from the active forces. As a result, modern MBTs now constitute half the assessed Soviet tank inventory, even though the total size of that inventory is declining. In the Atlantic-to-the-Urals (ATTU) zone, the area that will be affected by a CFE Treaty, the proportion of modern tanks is now nearly 70 percent of the total inventory. The increase of modern tanks from 1988 to 1990 is about 11 percent for the assessed total inventory and 24 percent for the ATTU zone. In addition to the production of new tanks, the Soviets and their East European allies have been improving the protective capabilities of their tanks with reactive armor packages, wraparound armor and side skirts, as well as bolt-on armor to protect turret tops and engine compartments.

Since unilateral measures were announced, and the CFE talks were begun, the Soviets have transferred a substantial amount of equipment east of the Urals outside the limitations area. About 7,000 tanks have been moved into storage depots outside the CFE limitations area. At the same time, only a comparatively modest number of systems has been destroyed or converted to civil use.

Soviet artillery modernization continues at an impressive rate. About one-third of the howitzers and guns deployed in active units in the ATTU zone now consist of modern, self-propelled systems. Soviet units are also being upgraded with the new M1983 multiple rocket launcher (MRL) system. Over one-fifth of MRLs deployed in units in the ATTU zone are now modern systems — 220-mm and greater — such as the BM-22 and the M1983. The Soviets also continue to upgrade their conventional munition stocks with improved con-

NOVOSTI/SOVFOTO

Complementing the Soviet fixed command post network used to direct complex, theater-level operations are an array of field-mobile command posts from which staffs direct lower-level, tactical operations.

ventional munitions, fuel-air explosives, enhanced blast technology, and subprojectile warheads. All of the new artillery systems can fire chemical rounds, and weapons 152-mm and above are also nuclear-capable.

Nearly half of all short-range ballistic missiles and rockets (with ranges less than 500 kilometers) remaining in Soviet Groups of Forces in Eastern Europe are now

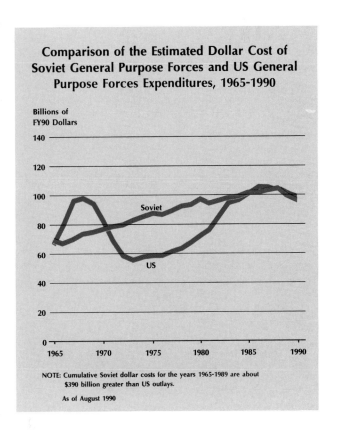

Comparison of the Estimated Dollar Cost of Soviet General Purpose Forces and US General Purpose Forces Expenditures, 1965-1990

Billions of FY90 Dollars

NOTE: Cumulative Soviet dollar costs for the years 1965-1989 are about $390 billion greater than US outlays.

As of August 1990

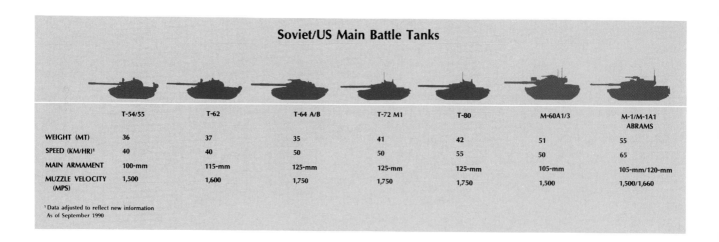

Soviet/US Main Battle Tanks

	T-54/55	T-62	T-64 A/B	T-72 M1	T-80	M-60A1/3	M-1/M-1A1 ABRAMS
WEIGHT (MT)	36	37	35	41	42	51	55
SPEED (KM/HR)[1]	40	40	50	50	55	50	65
MAIN ARMAMENT	100-mm	115-mm	125-mm	125-mm	125-mm	105-mm	105-mm/120-mm
MUZZLE VELOCITY (MPS)	1,500	1,600	1,750	1,750	1,750	1,500	1,500/1,660

[1] Data adjusted to reflect new information
As of September 1990

the modern SS-21 system. The Soviets have withdrawn more than the originally promised 24 short-range ballistic missile (SRBM) systems from Poland, Czechoslovakia, Hungary, and East Germany.

CONVENTIONAL AIR FORCES

The Soviet Air Force (SAF) comprises three major elements: the Air Armies of the Supreme High Command (VGK), Air Forces of the Military Districts and Groups of Forces (AF MD/GOF), and Military Transport Aviation (VTA). Since Gorbachev's December 1988 United Nations (UN) speech, there have been some dramatic air force changes, especially to those forces within the ATTU region. These changes include a significant reduction in combat aircraft and an increased rate of force modernization. The Soviets are retaining as much employment flexibility as possible through restructuring.

Air Armies of the Supreme High Command (VGK)

Despite aviation restructuring and reductions, the intermediate-range bomber force — assigned to attack deep theater targets — continues to modernize. Approximately 475 operational attack and support intermediate-range bombers are assigned to the Smolensk and Irkutsk Air Armies based in the western and far eastern regions of the USSR. Over 60 percent of the attack force has now been modernized. While some existing reconnaissance and electronic countermeasures (ECM) Badgers and Blinders have been reconfigured to enhance their capabilities, there has been no apparent effort to modernize substantially this portion of the force.

The supersonic Tu-22M Backfire intermediate-range bomber is steadily replacing obsolete Tu-16 Badger attack units. While Backfire units are smaller than those of Badger, the increased combat radius and supersonic

The new M1989 version of the Soviet T-80 main battle tank was paraded in Moscow this past spring.

Soviet Divisions: Equipment and Personnel Holdings[1]
(As of August 1990)

	Tank		Motorized Rifle Division (MRD)	
	Standard	New	Standard	New
Tanks	330	264	220[2]	162
APC/IFV	225	430	439	650
Artillery	165	190[1]	215	190
Personnel	11,100	13,500	13,500	16,000

[1] The Soviets have conducted major upgrades in the numbers and quality of their fire support mortars not included in this total.
[2] MRDs assigned to Groups of Forces (GOF) traditionally have 270 tanks assigned.

	2S1	2S3	2S5	2A36	2S7	2S19	M109A2/A3	M110A2	M198
TOWED/ SELF-PROPELLED	Self-Propelled	Self-Propelled	Self-Propelled	Towed	Self-Propelled	Self-Propelled	Self-Propelled	Self-Propelled	Towed
CALIBER/TYPE	122-mm Howitzer	152-mm Howitzer	152-mm Gun	152-mm Gun	203-mm Gun	152-mm Gun	155-mm Howitzer	203-mm Howitzer	155-mm Howitzer
MAXIMUM RANGE[1] (M)	15,000	18,000	28,500	28,500	35,000	Unknown	18,100	21,300	18,100
NUCLEAR-CAPABLE	No	Yes	Yes	Yes	Yes	Yes	Yes	Yes	Yes

[1] Ranges can be extended by the use of rocket-assisted projectiles.
As of September 1990

performance of this bomber greatly exceed those of the Badger. In addition, the recent deployment of a new short-range attack missile with the Backfire has significantly increased its potential weapons-carrying capability.

The combat power of the Legnica and Vinnitsa Air Armies lies mainly in 240 Su-24 Fencer light bombers. Since 1989, these Air Army forces diminished by almost 50 percent. Their numerical size was reduced through decreasing the size of subordinate regiments and resubordinating regiments to Soviet Naval Aviation (SNA) and to the AF MD/GOF. While the size of the Air Armies of the VGK has declined, the total number of Fencer light bombers in the Soviet forces has remained the same. In addition to the Fencers, these forces contain 200 fighters and 70 reconnaissance/electronic warfare (EW) aircraft. The fighter force has also been reduced, but, by the end of 1990, all of the aging MiG-21 Fishbeds and MiG-23 Floggers will have been replaced with Su-27 Flankers, or late-generation Floggers.

Frontal Aviation

The majority of the Soviet conventional aviation forces are assigned to the AF MD/GOF which, in wartime, will be assigned to various fronts to support ground operations and achieve frontal objectives. Particularly in the ATTU region, these are the forces most affected by the changes. The majority of the reductions, modernization, and restructuring have occurred within Frontal Aviation.

The reductions have been accomplished by decreasing the size of tactical combat regiments, removing entire regiments, and resubordinating aircraft to SNA and Aviation of Air Defense (APVO). The majority of the aircraft reduced from the inventory have been older Fishbeds, Floggers, and Su-17 Fitters. These reductions have affected both the strike assets and fighter force. The reconnaissance/EW force has been restructured with very little reduction of assets. The majority of the aircraft removed from the SAF inventory has been placed into storage or assigned to training schools. Approximately 290 Fencer, Fitter, Su-25 Frogfoot, and MiG-27 Flogger aircraft were transferred from the Air Force to Soviet Naval Aviation. Although reduced from the Air Force, nearly all of these aircraft continue to be assigned west of the Urals. An additional 200 Soviet aircraft are expected to be withdrawn from Hungary and Czechoslovakia by mid-1991. There is no indication that any destruction of aircraft has occurred or that the aircraft placed in storage will be destroyed in the near term. In CFE negotiations, NATO's position, in accordance with the agreed mandate, is that all land-based combat aircraft must be subject to treaty provisions, but the Soviets have insisted on excluding

NOVOSTI/SOVFOTO

A pair of Su-25 Frogfoots, the Soviet Air Force's twin-engine, subsonic, close air support fighter, banks across the horizon. The aircraft, used also in short-range interdiction missions, is armed with air-to-ground ordnance, including antitank rockets and missiles, and an internal twin-barrel 30-mm gun.

NOVOSTI/SOVFOTO

The Soviets are focusing their fighter production on the MiG-29 Fulcrum, seen here, and Su-27 Flanker. These aircraft have been demonstrated to be highly maneuverable, well-designed fighters capable of posing a serious air superiority threat to any opponent.

land-based Naval Aviation.

Concurrent with force reductions, the Soviets have undertaken a modernization program of these forces, particularly in the ATTU, with almost half of the regiments there receiving new or improved aircraft variants. In addition, modernization has been accompanied by some unilateral reductions and the relocation of existing aircraft. The Soviets have transferred portions or entire regiments to facilitate modernizing older regiments. Continuing new aircraft production also has supplemented their modernization program.

The Soviets are focusing their fighter production on the MiG-29 Fulcrum and Su-27 Flanker. These aircraft have been demonstrated to be highly maneuverable, well-designed fighters capable of posing a serious air superiority threat to any opponent. These existing production aircraft lag their US counterpart aircraft in avionics, weapons, and certain other features, but they are a much closer match than previous generations of Soviet aircraft. On the other hand, the Soviets have accepted much reduced production rates for the new aircraft, forcing a long-term decline in force size as older aircraft such as the Flogger leave the force in coming years. Meanwhile, the Soviets already are testing improved variants of the existing Fulcrum and Flanker that, when fielded, could reduce performance differences with US current aircraft by the mid-1990 timeframe. The prospect for entirely new follow-ons to the Flanker and Fulcrum sometime after the turn of the century remains a concern.

The Soviets are also restructuring their air forces in the ATTU region claiming this initiative constitutes a defensive posturing of the air forces. There have been some significant shifts in the force as a result of restructuring, most noticeably in Western TVD (WTVD) first echelon forces and in the Northwestern, Southwestern, and Southern TVDs. Within the WTVD's first echelon the Soviets created a defensive posture by removing half of their Fencer light bombers and changing the primary mission of two ground-attack regiments to air defense. This defensive restructuring was done at the expense of the second echelon forces which lost virtually all of their defensive fighter force, but gained significant numbers of offensive aircraft from the forward areas of the WTVD.

The flanks have changed disposition as well. In the Northwestern TVD, the three existing fighter-bomber regiments were removed; however, two were replaced with Fencers. In the Southwestern and Southern TVDs, most of the front-level ground-attack capability has been eliminated.

Soviet forces east of the Urals are effecting similar changes. The equivalent of nine regiments has been eliminated, primarily by reducing regimental sizes or disbanding units. Concurrent with this activity, four regiments of the most advanced fighter, ground-attack, and reconnaissance aircraft were introduced to upgrade older, less capable models.

Faced with significant cuts, the Soviets opted to retain their Fencer force, albeit in the rear areas, at the expense of their tactical fighter-bombers. To the Soviets, the Fencers represent a credible deterrent as well as a viable retaliatory force that can be quickly generated.

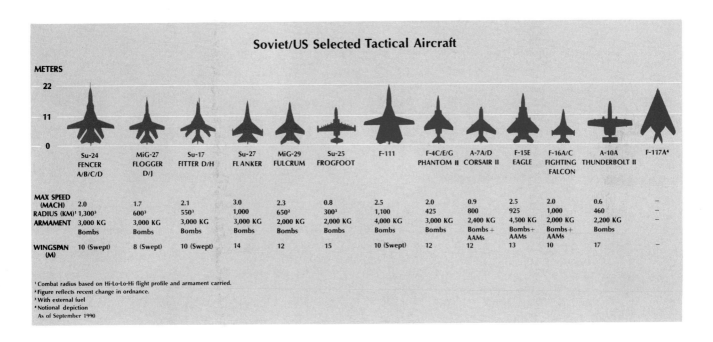

Soviet/US Selected Tactical Aircraft

	Su-24 FENCER A/B/C/D	MiG-27 FLOGGER D/J	Su-17 FITTER D/H	Su-27 FLANKER	MiG-29 FULCRUM	Su-25 FROGFOOT	F-111	F-4C/E/G PHANTOM II	A-7A/D CORSAIR II	F-15E EAGLE	F-16A/C FIGHTING FALCON	A-10A THUNDERBOLT II	F-117A[4]
MAX SPEED (MACH)	2.0	1.7	2.1	3.0	2.3	0.8	2.5	2.0	0.9	2.5	2.0	0.6	–
RADIUS (KM)[1]	1,300[3]	600[1]	550[3]	1,000	650[2]	300[3]	1,100	425	800	925	1,000	460	–
ARMAMENT	3,000 KG Bombs	3,000 KG Bombs	3,000 KG Bombs	3,000 KG Bombs	2,000 KG Bombs	2,000 KG Bombs	4,000 KG Bombs	3,000 KG Bombs	2,400 KG Bombs + AAMs	4,500 KG Bombs + AAMs	2,000 KG Bombs + AAMs	2,200 KG Bombs	–
WINGSPAN (M)	10 (Swept)	8 (Swept)	10 (Swept)	14	12	15	10 (Swept)	12	12	13	10	17	–

[1] Combat radius based on Hi-Lo-Lo-Hi flight profile and armament carried.
[2] Figure reflects recent change in ordnance.
[3] With external fuel
[4] Notional depiction
As of September 1990

The reductions to the fighter-bomber force significantly reduce the Soviets' capability for battlefield interdiction and direct fire support to their ground forces.

While the Soviet force in place now is qualitatively superior to that found a year ago, it has been reduced. Additionally, while the Soviets have given up much of their front-level offensive capability, they have created a strong forward air defense that improves their ability to protect their airspace. Additionally, they also have kept a significant offensive capability by retaining much of their deep-attack force in the Soviet Union.

Army Aviation

The Soviets continue to employ a variety of helicopters for direct combat and support roles. Attack helicopters such as the Mi-24 Hind and armed troop carrier versions of the Hip are now assigned to all Soviet tank/combined-arms armies. The Hind's wide range of machine guns and cannon, unguided rockets with a variety of warheads, and modern antitank guided missiles have been continually updated and improved since its initial appearance in the early 1970s, allowing a steady increase in battlefield performance with the same basic aircraft. A similar process has been applied to the Hip, with current models representing a quantum improvement in armament and performance over those first entering service in 1964. Hip also is found in command and electronic warfare support roles, while new models of the basic Hind for specialized reconnaissance roles are beginning to appear in quantity. Particular attention is being paid to increasing the wartime survivability of all these helicopters. A new generation of equipment providing active and passive protection against air defense threats is entering service, improving upon earlier versions used in Afghanistan.

Two new attack helicopters, the Mi-28 Havoc, which bears some resemblance to the US Apache, and the Kamov-designed Hokum, are expected to enter service with the Soviet military in 1991, after almost 10 years in development. The Havoc, although less effective than the Apache, will complement and eventually replace the Hind. It will be most capable in the type of close air support and antitank missions performed by Hind, and will be able to conduct air-to-air operations against enemy helicopters if required. Hokum is expected to have a primary air-to-air role against opposing helicopters and lower-performance fixed wing battlefield support aircraft, but will also have significant close air support capabilities. Increasing numbers of Havoc and Hokum entering service in the early 1990s, alongside the large number of Hinds and Hips already deployed, will provide the Soviets capable and responsive battlefield fire support across the full spectrum of offensive and defensive requirements.

Transport and other combat support helicopters also continue to modernize and improve. The replacement of the aging Mi-6 Hook (1960 service entry date) by the larger Mi-26 Halo transport helicopter has increased. Halos are now replacing Hooks on a one-for-one basis in transport helicopter regiments, rather than at a lesser ratio as earlier thought; this will significantly increase combat lift capability for resupply of air assault forces as well as routine logistics support. New variants of the Halo are likely in the early 1990s to begin to replace

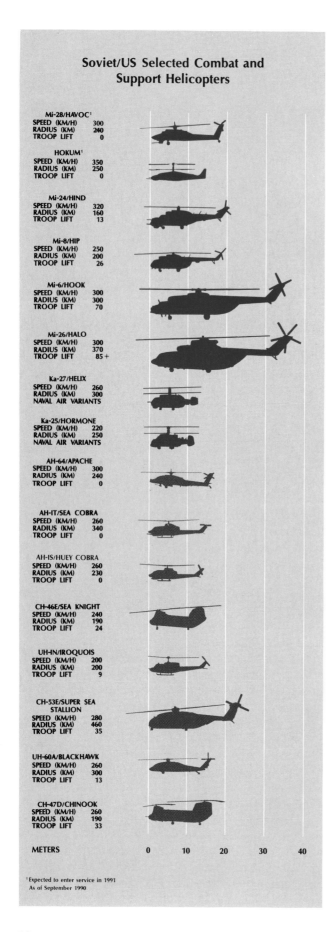

Soviet/US Selected Combat and Support Helicopters

Mi-28/HAVOC¹
SPEED (KM/H)	300
RADIUS (KM)	240
TROOP LIFT	0

HOKUM¹
SPEED (KM/H)	350
RADIUS (KM)	250
TROOP LIFT	0

Mi-24/HIND
SPEED (KM/H)	320
RADIUS (KM)	160
TROOP LIFT	13

Mi-8/HIP
SPEED (KM/H)	250
RADIUS (KM)	200
TROOP LIFT	26

Mi-6/HOOK
SPEED (KM/H)	300
RADIUS (KM)	300
TROOP LIFT	70

Mi-26/HALO
SPEED (KM/H)	300
RADIUS (KM)	370
TROOP LIFT	85 +

Ka-27/HELIX
SPEED (KM/H)	260
RADIUS (KM)	300
NAVAL AIR VARIANTS	

Ka-25/HORMONE
SPEED (KM/H)	220
RADIUS (KM)	250
NAVAL AIR VARIANTS	

AH-64/APACHE
SPEED (KM/H)	300
RADIUS (KM)	240
TROOP LIFT	0

AH-IT/SEA COBRA
SPEED (KM/H)	260
RADIUS (KM)	340
TROOP LIFT	0

AH-IS/HUEY COBRA
SPEED (KM/H)	260
RADIUS (KM)	230
TROOP LIFT	0

CH-46E/SEA KNIGHT
SPEED (KM/H)	240
RADIUS (KM)	190
TROOP LIFT	24

UH-IN/IROQUOIS
SPEED (KM/H)	200
RADIUS (KM)	200
TROOP LIFT	9

CH-53E/SUPER SEA STALLION
SPEED (KM/H)	280
RADIUS (KM)	460
TROOP LIFT	35

UH-60A/BLACKHAWK
SPEED (KM/H)	260
RADIUS (KM)	300
TROOP LIFT	13

CH-47D/CHINOOK
SPEED (KM/H)	260
RADIUS (KM)	190
TROOP LIFT	33

METERS   0   10   20   30   40

¹ Expected to enter service in 1991
As of September 1990

Hooks specialized for command support. Soviet tilt rotor prototypes should appear in the same timeframe, initially probably as a Hip replacement, and then larger models as the eventual successor to Halo.

NAVAL FORCES

In November 1985, then General Secretary Gorbachev selected Fleet Admiral V.N. Chernavin as Commander-in-Chief of the Soviet Navy, and since that time, the Navy has implemented reforms to make itself more efficient, stressed qualitative over quantitative values, continued its extensive modernization program, reduced its overseas presence, and emphasized operations more supportive of the USSR's declared "defensive doctrine."

The Soviet Navy's missions are quite different from those of the US Navy, or the navies of other major maritime nations. Primary Soviet missions are to:

- Operate and protect the Northern and Pacific Ocean Fleet strategic nuclear ballistic missile submarine (SSBN) force;
- Protect the seaward approaches of the Soviet Union from air, sea, or amphibious attack — especially from nuclear-capable enemy forces such as SSNs, aircraft carrier battle groups, air- and sea-launched cruise missiles and their launch platforms; and
- Support Soviet ground forces by securing contiguous maritime flanks, by providing naval fire and logistical support, conducting amphibious assaults, and disrupting enemy sea lines of communication.

The Soviet Navy intends to accomplish its principal missions by concentrating its SSBNs and the majority of its general purpose naval forces in waters relatively close to Soviet territory. Within these defensive areas, Soviet SSBNs and the maritime approaches to the Soviet Union are protected by an imposing array of nuclear- and diesel-powered attack submarines, surface combatants, and naval aircraft. These forces provide a formidable layered defense against external submarine, surface, and air threats.

Modernization and Construction

The Soviet Navy is engaged in a continuing modernization and construction program, with six new classes of attack submarines and seven classes of surface combatant warships having entered the inventory since 1980. This program is expected to continue well into the 1990s. Because of improved weapons systems, command, control, communications, and intelligence (C³I), and other sensors, the Soviet submarines and surface combatants

NOVOSTI/SOVFOTO

Two new attack helicopters, the Mi-28 Havoc, seen here, and the Kamov-designed Hokum, are expected to enter service with the Soviet military in 1991, after almost 10 years in development.

in production have capabilities far superior to those of their predecessors, largely offsetting the scrapping of obsolete surface and subsurface vessels.

The Soviet Union has embarked on an ambitious, long-term program to dismantle and scrap obsolescent naval ships, submarines, and eventually merchant ships and ocean-going fishing vessels. The result by 1996 is expected to be:

- The scrapping of up to 450 pre-1970s vintage combat ships, including about 45 general purpose submarines, and reduction of nearly 80,000 naval personnel, including both sea-going and shore support; and
- A smaller naval force, although qualitative improvements will make it a more capable one, and we anticipate little or no impairment of mission performance.

This scrapping program, in addition to providing economic gain for the Soviet Union, also is intended to contribute to reducing Western perceptions of the Soviet military threat. It will result in a smaller, but more reliable force, with reduced operation and mainte-nance costs and lower manpower requirements. Overall readiness and effectiveness may even increase, while Soviet Navy missions and operational concepts will be unaffected.

Submarines

The Soviet Navy's principal combatant is the sub-marine. Not surprisingly, the Soviets have the largest general purpose submarine force in the world. Newer submarines will continue to improve the force's capa-bilities with new designs that emphasize enhanced quieting, depth, weapon diversification, and sensors. Currently, four different classes of nuclear- or diesel-powered attack submarines are in series production.

Surface Combatants

Surface combatant production has been equally im-pressive. In 1989 the Soviets commenced sea trials of their first conventional takeoff-and-landing (CTOL) 65,000 metric-ton displacement guided-missile aircraft carrier (CVG), the first Tbilisi-class, Tbilisi. Another

CROWN

The employment of land-attack cruise missiles, such as the SS-N-21, by nuclear-powered attack submarines, including the *Akula*, shown here, will further enhance Soviet submarine nuclear force capabilities. These systems will probably be used against Eurasian theater strategic targets.

Tbilisi-class CVG, the Varyag (formerly Riga), is currently fitting out, and a follow-on 70,000 to 75,000 metric-ton displacement carrier is being constructed.

The Tbilisi is intended to accomplish forward air defense missions. The Tbilisi's airwing will likely consist of between 20 to 40 aircraft, including the Su-27 Flanker, MiG-29 Fulcrum, vertical/short takeoff and landing (VSTOL) aircraft, and helicopters. In addition to its airwing, the Tbilisi carries 12 SS-N-19 long-range antiship missiles (300-nm range), 24 launchers for 192 SA-N-9 short-range surface-to-air missiles, and for point defense, six AK-630 Gatling guns, and eight CADS-1 (combined air defense system-1) gun/missile systems.

The fourth modern Kirov-class nuclear-powered guided-missile cruiser (CGN) was launched in April 1989. The fifth cruiser was started in 1989 at Leningrad's Baltic Works, but work ceased soon thereafter. Further production of this class has been terminated. Production of the Slava-class guided-missile cruiser (CG) is continuing, very slowly. The launching of the fourth and probably last unit occurred in August 1990.

The largest destroyer program in the Soviet Navy since the 1950s was begun in 1980 with the advent of the Sovremennyy and Udaloy classes. The former is equipped mainly for antisurface warfare with eight SS-N-22 antiship cruise missiles, 40 SA-N-7 medium-range SAMs, and two twin 130-mm guns. The 8,200-ton Udaloy is oriented to antisubmarine warfare, carrying eight 55-kilometer range SS-N-14s, and capacity for 64 short-range SAMs (SA-N-9), and has two single-barrel 100-mm guns. The Navy has received 12 Sovremennyys and 10 more are in construction; the last of 12 Udaloys should enter service in 1991, and the first unit of a modified version of the class should enter the fleet in 1992. Completion of the Udaloy and Sovremennyy classes continues at the rate of about one per year for each class.

A number of frigate- and corvette-sized ships also continue to be built. Investment in these programs will guarantee that the Navy and the KGB Maritime Border Guard will have sufficient surface warfare, antisubmarine warfare, mine warfare, and coastal patrol capability well into the next century. Finally, the Soviet Navy's amphibious lift capability continues to modernize with the completion of the third Ivan Rogov amphibious assault transport dock (LPD). Smaller craft such as the Pomornik-class air cushioned landing craft, and a wing-in-ground effect craft are expected to join the fleet at a slow but steady rate.

Soviet Naval Aviation (SNA) Developments

The Soviets have long relied on land-based, and to a lesser extent seaborne, naval aviation to provide intermediate- and short-range strike, antisubmarine warfare (ASW), mine countermeasures (MCM), reconnaissance, targeting, and search and rescue (SAR) support. The current trend for SNA is to emphasize improvements to its short-range tactical aviation capability. In addition, the Backfire C intermediate-range bomber continues to enter the force, albeit at a reduced rate, while the aging Badger force is being reduced.

The Soviets are still modernizing their fixed-wing ASW force and are on the verge of deploying a jet amphibian (the largest ever built) for this mission.

The recent resubordination of numerous former Soviet Air Force fighter-bombers to several Soviet Fleet Air Forces, particulary in the Atlantic-to-the-Urals region, increases naval air peripheral antiship strike capabilities and support for amphibious warfare forces. The inclusion of naval aircraft under CFE counting rules remains an unresolved issue. Under the Soviet approach of excluding land-based naval aircraft from a conventional arms control agreement, these recent transfers would protect aircraft newly resubordinated to Fleet Air Forces from CFE limits on aircraft.

Elements of Soviet Naval Warfighting Strategy

Since the mid-1980s, the Soviets have been emphasizing operations closer to home waters. Three naval warfare considerations have necessitated this change. First, the Soviets had the need to strengthen their ability to protect SSBNs operating in the Barents Sea, Arctic Ocean, and Seas of Japan and Okhotsk. Second, they perceived a growing threat to the USSR from land-attack cruise-missile-equipped submarines operating from under the Polar ice cap. Third, the Soviets are emphasizing combined strategic air defense operations with Soviet Air Defense Forces working closely with the Soviet Navy to extend the depth and scope of air defense coverage.

Antisubmarine Warfare (ASW) Forces

The Soviets consider Western nuclear-powered attack submarines (SSNs) operating in or near Soviet bastion areas as the greatest threat to their deployed SSBN force. To protect the SSBNs, the Soviets intend to establish protective barriers of ships, submarines, aircraft, sensors, and weapons around SSBN operating areas.

Antisurface Warfare (ASUW) Forces

The destruction of enemy surface forces — particularly aircraft carriers and land-attack cruise missile platforms — is another objective of the Soviet Navy. This task would receive higher priority should these forces approach within striking distance of the Soviet Union during a conflict. The Soviets intend to destroy US and NATO surface forces by conducting coordinated air, surface, and subsurface attacks with their torpedo and cruise-missile-equipped submarines, land-based naval and air force strike aircraft, and surface warships.

Strategic Air Defense

In response to the perceived US air- and sea-launched cruise-missile threat, the Soviet Navy is becoming heavily involved in combined air defense operations with the Soviet Air Defense Forces. When it becomes operational, the Tbilisi-class CVG will contribute to this mission by extending the range from which carrier-capable Soviet interceptors, the Su-27 Flanker and/or the MiG-29 Fulcrum, will be able to operate. The Soviets believe that their existing air defense capability is inadequate to defend the maritime axes from carrier-based aircraft, strategic bombers, and the new land-attack, air- and sea-launched cruise missiles. Therefore, the Navy is expected to increase its emphasis on combined air defense operations to ensure all surface, subsurface, and aviation assets are effectively used. Moscow will also continue to attempt to limit Western capabilities through arms control negotiations.

Since spring 1989, some 275 first-line Su-17 Fitter, Su-24 Fencer, Su-25 Frogfoot, and MiG-27 Flogger

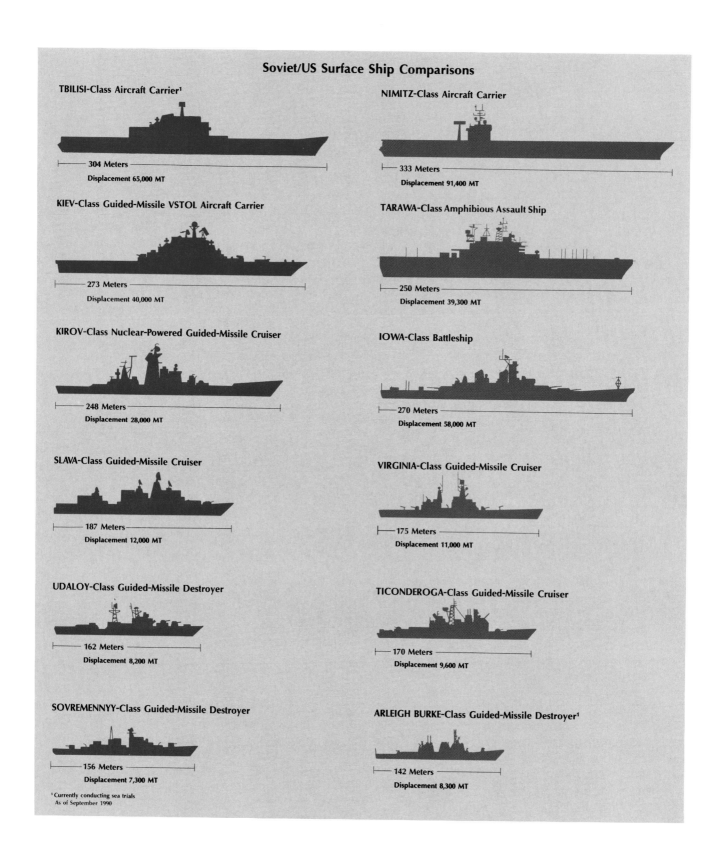

Soviet/US Surface Ship Comparisons

TBILISI-Class Aircraft Carrier[1]
304 Meters
Displacement 65,000 MT

NIMITZ-Class Aircraft Carrier
333 Meters
Displacement 91,400 MT

KIEV-Class Guided-Missile VSTOL Aircraft Carrier
273 Meters
Displacement 40,000 MT

TARAWA-Class Amphibious Assault Ship
250 Meters
Displacement 39,300 MT

KIROV-Class Nuclear-Powered Guided-Missile Cruiser
248 Meters
Displacement 28,000 MT

IOWA-Class Battleship
270 Meters
Displacement 58,000 MT

SLAVA-Class Guided-Missile Cruiser
187 Meters
Displacement 12,000 MT

VIRGINIA-Class Guided-Missile Cruiser
175 Meters
Displacement 11,000 MT

UDALOY-Class Guided-Missile Destroyer
162 Meters
Displacement 8,200 MT

TICONDEROGA-Class Guided-Missile Cruiser
170 Meters
Displacement 9,600 MT

SOVREMENNYY-Class Guided-Missile Destroyer
156 Meters
Displacement 7,300 MT

ARLEIGH BURKE-Class Guided-Missile Destroyer[1]
142 Meters
Displacement 8,300 MT

[1] Currently conducting sea trials
As of September 1990

land-based attack aircraft have been transferred to Soviet Naval Aviation. The newly received aircraft are believed to be intended primarily for a wartime maritime strike role in defense of Soviet territory. Land-based attack aircraft of both the Soviet Air Force and Soviet Naval Aviation have been performing an increased level of maritime strike activity over the last several years.

Soviet Attack Submarines

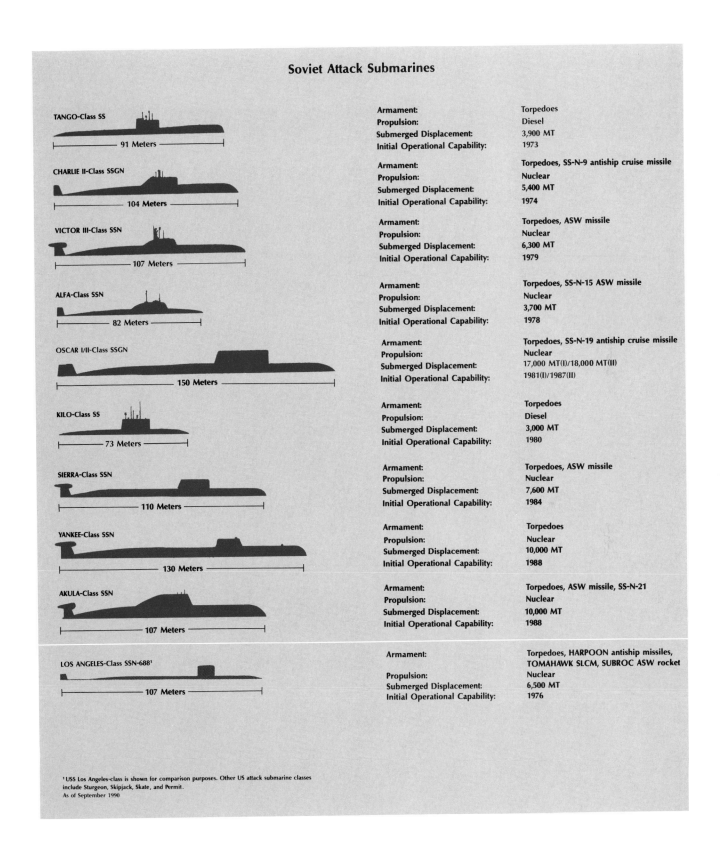

	Armament:	Torpedoes
TANGO-Class SS — 91 Meters	Propulsion:	Diesel
	Submerged Displacement:	3,900 MT
	Initial Operational Capability:	1973
CHARLIE II-Class SSGN — 104 Meters	Armament:	Torpedoes, SS-N-9 antiship cruise missile
	Propulsion:	Nuclear
	Submerged Displacement:	5,400 MT
	Initial Operational Capability:	1974
VICTOR III-Class SSN — 107 Meters	Armament:	Torpedoes, ASW missile
	Propulsion:	Nuclear
	Submerged Displacement:	6,300 MT
	Initial Operational Capability:	1979
ALFA-Class SSN — 82 Meters	Armament:	Torpedoes, SS-N-15 ASW missile
	Propulsion:	Nuclear
	Submerged Displacement:	3,700 MT
	Initial Operational Capability:	1978
OSCAR I/II-Class SSGN — 150 Meters	Armament:	Torpedoes, SS-N-19 antiship cruise missile
	Propulsion:	Nuclear
	Submerged Displacement:	17,000 MT(I)/18,000 MT(II)
	Initial Operational Capability:	1981(I)/1987(II)
KILO-Class SS — 73 Meters	Armament:	Torpedoes
	Propulsion:	Diesel
	Submerged Displacement:	3,000 MT
	Initial Operational Capability:	1980
SIERRA-Class SSN — 110 Meters	Armament:	Torpedoes, ASW missile
	Propulsion:	Nuclear
	Submerged Displacement:	7,600 MT
	Initial Operational Capability:	1984
YANKEE-Class SSN — 130 Meters	Armament:	Torpedoes
	Propulsion:	Nuclear
	Submerged Displacement:	10,000 MT
	Initial Operational Capability:	1988
AKULA-Class SSN — 107 Meters	Armament:	Torpedoes, ASW missile, SS-N-21
	Propulsion:	Nuclear
	Submerged Displacement:	10,000 MT
	Initial Operational Capability:	1988
LOS ANGELES-Class SSN-688[1] — 107 Meters	Armament:	Torpedoes, HARPOON antiship missiles, TOMAHAWK SLCM, SUBROC ASW rocket
	Propulsion:	Nuclear
	Submerged Displacement:	6,500 MT
	Initial Operational Capability:	1976

[1] USS Los Angeles-class is shown for comparison purposes. Other US attack submarine classes include Sturgeon, Skipjack, Skate, and Permit.
As of September 1990

Amphibious and Coastal Defense Operations

Traditionally, the primary mission of the estimated 18,000-man Soviet Naval Infantry (SNI) was to conduct limited amphibious operations in support of the maritime flanks of the ground forces. However, in line with defensive doctrine, the Soviets apparently have elevated SNI's formerly secondary mission of coastal defense.

TASS/SOVFOTO

One of two deck-edge elevators brings a MiG-29 Fulcrum to the flight deck of the Tbilisi-class aircraft carrier during flight operations in the Black Sea last year. The Tbilisi's airwing will likely consist of helicopters and between 20-to-40 Su-27 Flanker and MiG-29 Fulcrum aircraft.

Although the SNI continues to upgrade its mobility and firepower capabilities, it still retains the ability to conduct independent assaults or raids contiguous to ground force axes. SNI can also participate, if necessary, with ground and airborne forces in large-scale air-sea landing operations on the periphery of Eurasian theaters. SNI, however, is not configured for large-scale distant area combat.

Other Naval Operations

The naval missions of sea-lines-of-communication (SLOC) interdiction, amphibious operations against littoral countries, and offensive mining are not likely to have significant dedicated resources early in any conflict. Nevertheless, some level of effort would undoubtedly be made to disrupt NATO reinforcement and resupply capabilities within resource limitations. In a post-CFE environment, following the drawdown of US and Canadian forces in Central Europe with the requirement for massive troop deployments in any future conflict, it is possible that the Soviets could reevaluate and increase the priority of SLOC interdiction — particularly in a

protracted conflict.

The Soviets recognize the value of using unconventional forces for specialized offensive operations. The Soviets maintain a number of special operations forces for attacking high-value targets deep in enemy territory. Naval Special Purpose Forces, or Naval Spetsnaz, are operationally controlled by fleet intelligence directorates, and are located in each Soviet fleet area.

Naval Summary

The Soviet Navy's vital strategic forces, defensively oriented missions and strategy, and exclusion from current CFE negotiations, might place it in a better position than the other branches of the Soviet armed forces to weather Gorbachev's program of defense drawdowns. Despite some reductions in operating tempo, out-of-area deployments, and changes in force structure, Soviet naval missions remain virtually unchanged. Current modernization programs, if successful, could make the Soviet Navy a smaller yet qualitatively more capable force while projecting a less threatening image abroad.

TBILISI-CLASS AIRCRAFT CARRIER

The Tbilisi-class aircraft carrier, which departed its building yard in late 1989, continues to conduct sea trials and is not expected to deploy to the Soviet Northern Fleet until late 1990 or 1991.

Having demonstrated the ability to operate Su-27 Flanker, MiG-29 Fulcrum, and Su-25 Frogfoot aircraft from the ship, the Soviet Navy has clearly taken a significant step forward in the realm of shipborne tactical aviation. It is still too early to determine whether both Fulcrum and Flanker aircraft will be embarked in the carrier's established air wing or whether these aircraft remain in competition for the carrier role. The two-seater Frogfoot will be employed as a carrier-associated training aircraft. Tbilisi operations have confirmed the use of the bow ramp for take-off since the ship has no catapults. It has arresting gear for aircraft recovery.

The second unit of the class, Varyag (formerly Riga), continues to fit out in the Black Sea shipyard, and the lead ship of a larger follow-on class is under construction.

TASS/SOVFOTO

The sweeping, ski-jump bow of the new Tbilisi-class aircraft carrier makes it the first class of Soviet carriers capable of over-the-bow launches of conventional, fixed-wing aircraft. The Tbilisi carries 12 SS-N-19 long-range, vertically launched antiship missiles forward with flush-deck missile hatches on the bow deck.

CHEMICAL AND BIOLOGICAL WARFARE

During 1990 there has been notable progress in US/USSR chemical weapon (CW) negotiations. The late 1989 bilateral CW data exchange was followed by a series of exchange visits to CW facilities. On June 1, President Bush and President Gorbachev signed a CW destruction agreement calling for elimination of the vast bulk of US and Soviet stockpiles. The agreement calls for a start of the CW destruction process in 1992 and a reduction to 5,000 agent-tons by the year 2002.

In spite of these promising developments, the USSR continues to possess the most extensive CW capability in the world. Its stockpile, the world's largest, includes chemical agents in weapons and in bulk storage containers. The Soviets can deliver chemical agents with almost all of their conventional weapon systems, from mortars to short-range ballistic missiles to high performance aircraft. They have admitted that their inventory includes persistent and nonpersistent nerve agents, as well as blister agents. This variety of agents and delivery means allows the Soviets to select weapon systems that can effectively attack and neutralize virtually any target at any tactical range.

Specially trained and equipped troops enhance Soviet capabilities to protect themselves against potential nuclear, biological, and chemical (NBC) hazards. The Soviets have over 30,000 dedicated personnel specializing in reconnaissance and decontamination operations and over 30,000 special vehicles for NBC operations. Reorganization and restructuring, coupled with an effective training program, have improved the readiness of these troops to conduct sustained operations in a contaminated environment — be it a battlefield of the future or an industrial accident involving a nuclear or chemical facility. This protective capability enhances the Soviet potential to support offensive operations.

The Soviets face enormous problems in dealing with the destruction of their large chemical weapons inventory. They will probably begin by eliminating their old, obsolete systems that they showed to international visitors at Shikhany in 1987. During 1989, the newly constructed Soviet chemical weapons destruction facil-

Here, a chemical bomb is readied for dismantlement. The Soviets face enormous problems in dealing with the destruction of their large chemical weapons inventory. They will probably begin by eliminating obsolete systems such as those they showed to international visitors at Shikhany in 1987.

ity at Chapayevsk was a subject of concern to Soviet journalists and environmentalists. Neighboring residents demonstrated at the facility throughout the spring and summer protesting that the site was unsafe and would create environmental hazards. US congressmen who visited the site in August 1989 were apprehensive about the level of technology the Soviets were planning to use to destroy nerve agent weapons. Safety provisions were noticeably lacking at the plant. A few weeks after the visit, the Soviets announced the "conversion" of the Chapayevsk facility — saying it would become a training site to study industrial methods of eliminating toxic agents.

The Soviets lack the capability to destroy their chemical weapon stocks in an efficient, safe manner. The June 1990 CW Destruction Accord offers the Soviets US technical assistance that will enable them to proceed with destruction plans while negotiations toward the multilateral Chemical Weapons Convention continue.

Although Moscow denies that an offensive biological warfare (BW) program exists, the Soviets continue to improve biological technologies, including genetic engineering, which are being harnessed to improve the toxicity, stability, and military potential of the Soviet BW stocks. There has been evidence not only to support the existence of Soviet BW research and development, but also weaponized agents. The 1979 Sverdlovsk biological agent accident that resulted in the release of anthrax from a BW institute provided some of the evidence that the Soviets have violated the Biological Weapons Convention (BWC) of 1972.

During the past year, the Soviets have waged a campaign to add monitoring provisions to the BWC. It is possible that they are now going to allow visits to some of their "secret" facilities in order to alleviate Western concerns about BWC-forbidden activity at these sites. However, illegal activity could easily be transferred to alternate locations. Even with stringent monitoring provisions, it would be nearly impossible to reliably assess compliance with the BWC.

RADIO-ELECTRONIC COMBAT (REC)

The Soviets continue to upgrade their capability to disrupt the command and control of Western military forces. Embodied in the doctrine known as Radio-Electronic Combat (REC) is an integrated effort which includes elements of reconnaissance, electronic countermeasures (jamming), physical disruption (destruction), and deception. Each element contributes to the disruption of enemy command and control at critical decision points in battle. REC forces continue to undergo modernization and expansion to serve as a force multiplier within a reorganized, numerically smaller, combat force.

Recent additions of REC capabilities to Soviet ground forces demonstrate an increasing reliance upon this element of their warfighting arsenal. New, more capable intercept and direction-finding systems as well as advanced jamming systems continue to be fielded within Soviet divisions, armies, and military districts.

The increase in REC forces has been supported by a major increase in the number of conscripts trained as REC system operators. The emphasis placed on this effort highlights the Soviet belief that REC will provide Soviet forces with an advantage by preventing the enemy commander from effectively controlling his forces, during battle. This advantage has become critical as Soviet forces have become smaller and have been forced to rely more on their technical capabilities rather than numerical superiority.

The technically advanced, robust REC structure present in the Soviet ground forces is mirrored by advances being made within the REC-associated elements of all the Soviet services. New jamming aircraft and more capable naval-associated jamming systems are being introduced into the services' inventory. These actions highlight the increasing reliance being placed on REC in an environment of diminishing force size.

LOGISTICS

The restructuring and reductions in Warsaw Pact

forces are beginning to be reflected in the logistic support structure. The change to smaller, more modern, better-equipped combat forces ultimately is expected to result in smaller, more capable logistic support units. The overall materiel sustainability of Soviet and East European forces will probably remain at current high levels. However, the withdrawal to Soviet territory of large quantities of supplies currently stored in the Forward Area inevitably will increase the time required to return supportable, sustainable forces to Eastern Europe should the need arise and create some short-term dislocations in the Soviet Union as the process continues.

Ground Forces Logistics

During the past decade, the Warsaw Pact developed a ground forces logistic structure that could effectively support simultaneous strategic offensives in multiple theaters of military operations. Improvements were made in sustainability of the combat force, and the survivability, mobility, efficiency, and standardization of logistic support elements. While the changes currently under way will probably modify Warsaw Pact logistic support concepts, they have not yet significantly reduced the materiel sustainability of ground forces.

Reductions in logistic stocks and support units have lagged behind reductions in combat units. Nondivisional stocks have not yet been reduced. These stocks constitute the bulk of the supplies stored in the Forward Area and include large quantities of items such as bridging systems, spare parts, and supplies.

Under the troop withdrawal agreements with Czechoslovakia and Hungary, it appears that the logistic stocks and support units will be among the last Soviet elements to be withdrawn. Most of the ammunition withdrawn will probably be placed in storage in the Soviet Union. Petroleum, oil, and lubricants (POL) supplies may be sold or bartered to East European military forces or civilian economies, or returned to the USSR and placed in military or civilian reserve stores.

Logistic support concepts also appear to be changing. The traditional concept centralizes most supplies and support units at front level. At the CSCE/CSBM Military Doctrine Seminar in January 1990, several Warsaw Pact nations indicated that storage at central depots was being reduced in favor of increased storage at division level. Decentralizing the ground forces logistic system could make supplies and support units less vulnerable and provide lower-level commanders with more reliable support during defensive operations.

Air Forces Logistics

Although some movement of munition and POL stocks has been seen recently, there have apparently been no major reductions in Forward Area stocks supporting air units. Large stocks of weapons and POL are deployed forward with or near combat regiments. These stocks have increased significantly over the past decade, and storage facilities have become more survivable. The Soviet Air Forces' main operating bases have become more modern, with substantial increases in hardened aircraft bunkers and POL storage capacity, and runway enhancement.

The Soviet aircraft maintenance program allows their air forces to maintain regiments at a high state of combat readiness. Soviet fighter and fighter-bomber regiments routinely maintain a high percentage of their aircraft at combat readiness, due in part to low annual flying hours by combat aircraft. The ongoing Soviet reorganization has enhanced maintenance and readiness by eliminating older airframes which required more maintenance and reducing the number of aircraft in a regiment, thus reducing the maintenance workload. Aircraft designed to simplify maintenance tasks, such as the comparatively simple Su-25 Frogfoot attack aircraft, and the commonality of weapon systems also contribute to maintaining high readiness levels.

Although this logistic system provides adequate support for Soviet Air Forces in peacetime, it has shortcomings. In particular, Soviet aircraft maintenance relies heavily on scheduled maintenance routines and low numbers of annual flying hours. It is unclear whether Soviet ground crews could deal with the maintenance demands encountered during high intensity air combat, particularly without a formal aircraft battle damage capability.

Naval Forces Logistics

Historically, the Soviet Navy has had several deficiencies in its logistic support structure, particularly in support of deployed forces. The Navy has placed a low priority on under-way at-sea replenishment and munitions transfer. To overcome some of these difficulties, the Navy supplements fleet auxiliaries by relying on tankers from the Soviet Merchant Fleet to provide fuel and obtain supplies in Western ports for deployed naval combatants.

As the Navy continues to reduce their out-of-area presence, the burden on the logistic support structure will be lessened. In addition, the scrapping and selling of older ships and submarines will reduce the burden of maintaining outdated units and enable the Navy to focus its resources elsewhere. Overall, this should allow the Navy support infrastructure to function more efficiently.

While the Soviets have decreased their out-of-area presence, they continue to use a number of foreign ship repair facilities. The primary Soviet motive for using these facilities is political in nature, and not the quality of work accomplished at these facilities. In this fashion, the Soviets hope to gain some degree of leverage in countries that depend on ship repair work.

STRATEGIC MOBILITY

The modernization of Military Transport Aviation (Voyenno Transportnaya Aviatsiya or VTA) has continued apace, despite other reductions and restructuring. Replacement of the medium-range, four-engine turboprop An-12 Cub by the more capable long-range Il-76 Candid jet transport has led to a steady increase in lift capacity for the VTA.

An-124 Condors, almost all of which are subordinated to VTA, have been prominent in the West and Third World, flying support missions transporting heavy and bulky cargoes for a variety of customers. They have been involved in relatively little military-related cargo activity, but their military potential remains high.

Since early 1988, the VTA has been heavily involved in supporting Soviet efforts to cope with civil unrest in the Soviet republics. Both Candids and Cocks have been used to lift airborne forces and Ministry of Internal Affairs (MVD) troops to and from trouble spots on minimal notice. These operations have been well executed, and are further proof of the VTA's capabilities

and importance to the Soviets.

The USSR's civil aviation organization, Aeroflot, is the world's largest airline. Aeroflot is organized to transition quickly to a wartime role. Upon mobilization, it would serve as a primary means of troop transport, freeing military aircraft to transport equipment and cargo.

Soviet merchant fleet lift capability has grown during the past several years, as older, smaller ships have been replaced with larger, more specialized vessels. The Soviets have begun to buy used ships, to use flags of convenience, and have signed agreements which will permit manning Western ships with Soviet crews. This will give the Soviets access to ports where their own ships are not allowed. The increasingly large fleet of barge carriers, lighterage, and roll-on/roll-off ships gives the Soviets an improved capability to respond rapidly to military requirements in coastal areas, and to resupply troops over the shore.

REGIONAL MILITARY BALANCES

As a result of the sweeping changes occurring throughout Europe and within the Soviet Union, traditional assessments of the East-West balance must now place greater emphasis on political, economic, and historical factors. Although past capability indicators remain a critical measure of relative military capability, during the current period of instability these other factors have assumed even greater importance. This section addresses the regional implications of the changing capabilities and force structures that are emerging as a result of traditional and numerous new nonmilitary factors bringing about change in Europe and elsewhere. The key elements of change, as discussed earlier in this

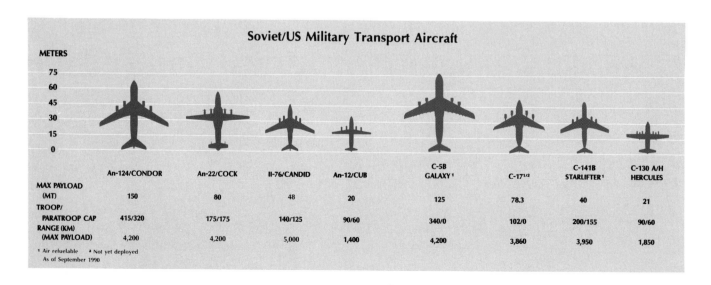

Soviet/US Military Transport Aircraft

METERS	An-124/CONDOR	An-22/COCK	Il-76/CANDID	An-12/CUB	C-5B GALAXY [1]	C-17 [1/2]	C-141B STARLIFTER [1]	C-130 A/H HERCULES
MAX PAYLOAD (MT)	150	80	48	20	125	78.3	40	21
TROOP/ PARATROOP CAP	415/320	175/175	140/125	90/60	340/0	102/0	200/155	90/60
RANGE (KM) (MAX PAYLOAD)	4,200	4,200	5,000	1,400	4,200	3,860	3,950	1,850

[1] Air refuelable   [2] Not yet deployed
As of September 1990

92

chapter, are applied to assessments of the US-Soviet balance.

The Soviet military establishment remains by far the most formidable on the Eurasian continent, although its capability to conduct offensive operations has recently declined after a long period of increase. The decline is most substantial in Europe, where the forces of other members of the Warsaw Pact appear no longer available for Soviet purposes. Reductions of Soviet forces have diminished Soviet advantages opposite Europe, Southwest Asia, and China.

Europe

The virtual dissolution of the Warsaw Pact as an alliance capable of combined offensive military operations and the initiation of major Soviet force reductions have produced a significant, favorable change in the European military balance. Following the 1989-90 political revolutions in Eastern Europe, new governments are now obtaining the withdrawal of Soviet forces from their territory. Consequently, almost all Soviet forces will likely be removed from Czechoslovakia and Hungary by mid-summer of 1991, and all but 48,000 from Poland by the end of 1991. Soviet units may remain in the eastern part of a united Germany until 1994. The German Democratic Republic (GDR) armed forces, until recently the most highly capable NSWP fighting force, will eventually be substantially reduced and incorporated into a unified German Territorial Army. Poland, Hungary, and Czechoslovakia are reducing their forces, adopting defense postures independent of Moscow, and rapidly reducing their cooperative activities with the Soviet forces in their countries. The Soviets could not count on Eastern European states to support an attack against the West.

The Abrams M-1A1 main battle tank, work horse of the US armored force, has a 120-mm smooth bore gun, improved armor, and the commander's independent thermal viewer (CITV) in its latest variants.

Coincident with extensive Soviet ground and air force withdrawals detailed earlier in the chapter, Moscow is also accelerating its withdrawal of short-range nuclear forces (SNF). The Soviets have announced they will reduce their forces in Eastern Europe by 60 nuclear missile launchers and 1,500 nuclear munitions. The United States has announced that it will forego modernization of its ground-based SNF missile systems. At their July 1990 summit in London, the Allies decided that once SNF negotiations begin, the NATO Alliance

The US Air Force's F-117A stealth fighter is the world's first operational aircraft designed to exploit low observable stealth technology for attack missions in dense threat environments.

Status of Soviet and Warsaw Pact Forces In Eastern Europe

WESTERN GROUP OF FORCES (WGF)[1] / EAST GERMANY[2]

Withdrawn	Remaining	Disbanded	Remaining
2 TDs	9 TDs		2 TDs
	8 MRDs		4 MRDs
2400 Tanks	5440 Tanks		5 MOB MRDs
		44 Tanks	2952 Tanks

SOUTHERN GROUP OF FORCES (SGF)[3] / HUNGARY

Withdrawn	Remaining	Disbanded	Remaining
2 TDs		2 Tank Brigades	3 Tank Brigades
	2 MRDs	2 MR Brigades	10 MR Brigades
962 Tanks	305 Tanks	1 Tank Brigade is converting to MR Brigade	
		320 Tanks	1010 Tanks

NORTHERN GROUP OF FORCES (NGF) / POLAND

Withdrawn	Remaining	Disbanded	Remaining
	1 TD	TDs and MRDs are converting to MDs	9 MDs
	1 MRD	3 MOB MRDs	4 MOB MRDs
94 Tanks	600 Tanks	420 Tanks	3000 Tanks

CENTRAL GROUP OF FORCES (CGF)[4] / CZECHOSLOVAKIA

Withdrawn	Remaining	Disbanded	Remaining
1 TD	1 TD	5 TRs	5 TDs
1 MRD	2 MRDs		5 MRDs
644 Tanks	811 Tanks		5 MOB MRDs
		100 Tanks	3955 Tanks

BULGARIA / ROMANIA

Disbanded	Remaining	Disbanded	Remaining
	9 MRDs	None	8 MRDs
1 Tank Brigade	4 Tank Brigades		2 TDs
138 Tanks	1,998 Tanks		1,949 Tanks

[1] The Kohl-Gorbachev agreement of 16 July 90 stated that WGF will withdraw over a three to four year period.
[2] Structure and compostion of East German military subject to German unification
[3] Moscow has agreed to withdraw all forces from Hungary by June 1991.
[4] Moscow has agreed to withdraw all forces from Czechoslovakia by July 1991.
As of September 1990

TD = Tank Division
TR = Tank Regiment
MRD = Motorized Rifle Division
MR = Motorized Rifle
MOB = Mobilized Status - 5 percent manning
MD = Mechanized Division

will propose, in return for reciprocal action by the Soviet Union, the elimination of all of its nuclear artillery shells from Europe.

The Soviets continue to improve the forces in their flank TVDs. They are transferring equipment, especially aircraft, from the central to the flank regions, increasing the capabilities of Soviet forces opposite NATO's northern and southern flanks. Of particular note, MiG-27 fighter-bombers have been transferred recently from Hungary to the Kola Peninsula. It is not clear whether this activity is a conscious Soviet strategy or a result of the restructuring that is occurring as the Soviets manage the withdrawals from the central region. Of equal concern is the fact that these aircraft have been transferred from the Air Force to the Navy, which would exempt them from CFE under the Soviets' approach of excluding land-based naval air from treaty limits.

These withdrawals and reductions, when added to the extensive reductions ongoing and planned in the Soviet Union, will diminish substantially Soviet advantages opposite Europe and other regions of the world. However, these quantitative trends favorable to NATO, and the quantitative parity that CFE would achieve for certain types of equipment, are not the only important factors in shaping the military balance. The ability to compete technologically, deploy rapidly, and sustain forces over a period of hostility are also critical determinants of military capability.

Modernization

The Soviets are scaling back their military procurement, which fell about 8 percent in 1989 from 1988 levels, with tanks and aircraft incurring the greatest cuts. These reduced procurement rates, however, will still support a brisk pace of modernization for the significantly reduced and restructured post-CFE Soviet forces. For example, in 1989, Soviet tank production declined dramatically, but remains greater than that of all the NATO nations combined. Soviet procurement of large mortars, air defense artillery systems, and lighter armored vehicles actually increased.

Maintaining and modernizing CFE-permitted force levels will be difficult for NATO states in the face of pressures to reduce their defense spending dramatically. This could result in a more rapid rate of modernization on the Soviet side, unless (as is possible) Soviet economic difficulties bring about further Soviet procurement reductions. In fact, the Soviets have recently indicated that arms production would be cut further in 1991.

Readiness and Sustainability

CFE limits will make reserve force readiness and overall force sustainability increasingly important to both sides. Once CFE-mandated force limits are reached, the Soviets' ability to generate large additional forces relatively quickly would depend, to a significant extent, on the condition of its strategic reserves east of the Urals. The Soviets are moving large amounts of ground weapon systems from the ATTU region to areas east of the Urals, placing them in storage depots that are outside the geographic limits of the prospective CFE agreement. They currently have over 7,000 tanks and over 12,000 pieces of probable CFE-Treaty-limited artillery stored in these depots.

Additionally, approximately 300 older MiG-23 Flogger and Su-17 Fitter aircraft from the ATTU have been placed in storage east of the Urals. The Soviets have built parking aprons, which is unusual, but they do not appear to have prepared the aircraft for long-term storage.

The Soviets' ability to maintain both this large quantity of equipment in prolonged storage, and a trained manpower base to operate it, will be important in determining the effect of this repositioning activity on the military balance.

The Soviets recently provided information on their logistic stockpiles in Eastern Europe. The USSR maintains up to 40 days of ammunition and fuel supplies in the GDR, Poland, Hungary, and Czechoslovakia. The condition of these supplies is unknown.

Only a few NATO countries have been able to meet the Alliance's standards for reserve stocks of fuel and ammunition. Ammunition shortfalls are more serious, especially with respect to modern munitions. This condition may be mitigated somewhat by the anticipated reduction in force levels; however, the increased premium placed on mobile operations would increase demands on NATO's fuel stocks.

If the Soviets withdraw their ammunition and POL stocks as they pull their forces back from Eastern Europe, the time required for Moscow to project sustainable forces back into the area will increase. Bulk logistic supplies would make up a large part of the total tonnage required to be moved by rail and road during a Soviet return of forces to Eastern Europe. In addition, the lack of modern materiel-handling equipment and containerization in the Soviet logistic system makes loading and transloading of bulk supplies extremely time- and manpower-intensive. However, unless the Soviets eliminate significant quantities of supplies in the wake of a CFE agreement, their sustainability advantage over NATO will likely increase as the size of NATO and Soviet forces decreases.

With respect to manpower and mobilization, NATO ground force reserves are generally more capable of quickly attaining their wartime readiness levels than are their Soviet counterparts. NATO also enjoys an advantage in that, with the exception of US and Canadian forces, its reservist forces are located relatively closer to their units and the likely focal point of conflict. Soviet units located throughout the USSR are dependent on the mobilization of large numbers of reservists, and

SOVIET AND EAST EUROPEAN FORCE REDUCTIONS AND RESTRUCTURING

The Soviets originally had planned to unilaterally withdraw six tank divisions and 5,300 tanks from Eastern Europe by the end of 1990. Four tank divisions were to have been withdrawn from the Western Group of Forces (WGF) in East Germany and one tank division each from the Central Group of Forces (CGF) in Czechoslovakia and the Southern Group of Forces (SGF) in Hungary. However, these withdrawal plans have been overtaken by the rapid pace of events in Eastern Europe. The new Czechoslovak and Hungarian Governments negotiated with Moscow the early withdrawal of Soviet forces from their territories by mid-1991. Now the Soviets have committed themselves to withdrawing five more divisions, 113,000 more personnel, and 1,000 more tanks from Eastern Europe earlier than they had planned. The withdrawal of Soviet Forces from East German territory was suspended, but the Gorbachev-Kohl agreement included a Soviet commitment to withdraw all of its forces from East German territory by 1994. In addition, the Polish Government, which had previously indicated a desire to retain Soviet forces until its western borders were assured, has agreed to negotiations on the eventual withdrawal of all but 48,000 Soviet troops.

Despite the uncertain political situation in Europe and the focus on negotiated withdrawals and progress toward a conventional arms agreement, Warsaw Pact unilateral reductions continue. The Soviets have maintained progress towards meeting their original announced reductions from the Atlantic-to-the-Urals (ATTU) zone.

Many Soviet spokesmen have mentioned that improvements in equipment quality and unit readiness will accompany reductions to maintain significant capabilities in the residual force structure. Concurrently, 46 divisions, including those deployed in the groups of forces, have begun some type of reorganization or have been upgraded in two or more combat systems; 20 other divisions have received one new weapon system. Eighty-five percent of the reorganized and upgraded units are in the ATTU zone.

Restructuring the Soviet Air Forces in the Far East is under way and expected to continue through 1990. To date, the Soviets have disbanded completely four fixed-wing tactical combat air regiments, including one in Mongolia. Other regiments have undergone partial cuts in strength. The result is a 22 percent reduction of regional tactical aircraft.

Long-term modernization of tactical air forces is continuing. Two Su-24/Fencer E squadrons and the first MiG-29/Fulcrum regiments were assigned along the Chinese border in 1989. Bomber and strategic interceptor units remain unaffected by the restructuring effort.

To date the Soviets have withdrawn unilaterally from Eastern Europe four divisions and over 3,600 tanks. As the withdrawals have taken place, the remaining divisions have been reorganized into the more defensive structure described above.

Most of the 10,000 tanks and all of the artillery pieces have been removed from the ATTU as promised (either by destruction, conversion, relocation to east of the Urals or exportation). At least 29 divisions have been disbanded or deactivated, the headquarters of at least eight armies or army corps have been eliminated, and military districts have been reduced from 16 to 14. When the withdrawals and reductions have been completed, the Soviet ground forces will have fewer divisions, armies, and military districts and less tanks. They hope to become a more modern, efficient force overall.

it will take longer to deploy them after mobilization. Furthermore, opposition to the draft is rapidly growing within several Soviet republics. Several recent incidents of no-shows and major shortfalls in draft call-ups reflect this trend. If this attitude becomes widespread, the Soviets' ability to effect a rapid and complete mobilization of their forces may be suspect.

Implications for Europe

Until recently, Soviet military doctrine focused on a combined theater strategic offensive designed to penetrate deeply into Western Europe and cripple or destroy NATO. In the wake of East European developments and Soviet force reductions, the Soviets probably consider an attack of this type highly risky, with little prospect for success. While in the past Soviet military doctrine described a theater strategic offensive as the preferred means of repelling attack, their new doctrine envisions conducting a strategic defensive operation to wear down an attacker while providing Moscow time to mobilize reserve forces for counteroffensive operations. The "counteroffensive" capabilities the Soviets retain will be an important determinant of their future capacity for offensive war, and will be a function of Soviet practices regarding modernization, readiness, and sustainability (including storage of equipment withdrawn from ATTU).

If the Soviet Union did decide to initiate war in Europe, reduced Soviet standing forces and a potentially hostile Eastern Europe would make it likely that Soviet attack objectives would be much more limited than those envisioned in the past. A full-scale Soviet attack toward NATO would require an extensive period of mobilization. However, the Soviet Union, even with no mobilization, remains militarily far superior to any single European country.

Middle East/Southwest Asia

The Soviets have been reducing their forces in the Southern TVD (STVD) over the past two years. With the Soviet withdrawal from Afghanistan, Soviet ground forces assigned to the STVD were reduced from roughly 30 divisions to around 25. STVD forces also included one airborne division, and 18 fighter and fighter-bomber regiments (with over 700 tactical aircraft) located in the North Caucasus, Transcaucasus, and Turkestan Military Districts (MDs). In June 1989, a reorganization consolidated two MDs, adding nine extant ground divisions and several fighter and fighter-bomber regiments to STVD High Command forces. These are not new forces, but they have become more directly available for the Southwest Asia theater. The Soviets have claimed that a total of 60,000 troops will be withdrawn from elements in the southern USSR by the beginning of 1991. That reduction was probably completed when forces withdrawn from Afghanistan were either demobilized or moved out of the region and units in the Turkestan MD were deactivated or disbanded.

Soviet forces in the STVD have consistently been maintained at a lower level of readiness than Soviet forces opposite Europe. However, even with these extensive reductions, the Soviet force structure in the STVD would remain much more sizeable than that of any other country in the region.

The average Soviet naval strength in the Mediterranean Sea is 25-35 ships. The Soviets have limited access to naval facilities in Syria, Libya, Tunisia, Algeria, and Yugoslavia. Additionally, Soviet Naval Aviation aircraft make periodic deployments to Syria and Libya. Soviet naval forces in the Indian Ocean average 12-15 ships. Regional naval support facilities available to the Soviets include the Island of Socotra and the Port of Aden in Yemen, and a facility on the Dahlak Islands of Ethiopia.

The US military presence in the region is comprised of the Sixth Fleet in the Mediterranean Sea, naval units in the Indian Ocean and Persian Gulf, and forces of the US Central Command (USCENTCOM). USCENTCOM forces on station in the Middle East/Southwest Asia region routinely include a command ship and four combatants. This force was substantially expanded in 1987 with the deployment of the Joint Task Force Middle East. US regional forces were reduced following the Iran-Iraq cease-fire in 1988, but are again being augmented in response to Iraqi aggression.

Direct intervention with conventional forces by either superpower has become far more difficult as a result of the dramatic increase in the military capabilities of regional states. Increased numbers of highly advanced military technologies, both conventional and unconventional, have proliferated throughout the military forces of the region. The Saudi acquisition of the Chinese CSS-2 Intermediate-Range Ballistic Missile (IRBM) is only the most recent and highly visible example of regional missile proliferation; a number of other states including Syria, Iraq, Israel, Pakistan, and India, also have ballistic missile capabilities. Furthermore, widespread Iraqi use of chemical weapons and Iranian retaliation in kind may have lowered the threshold for chemical weapon use throughout the region. Nuclear weapons may already be in the arsenals of several regional states.

Implications for Middle East/Southwest Asia

The ethnic violence in the Soviet Transcaucasus is one indication of the severity and complexity of the problems facing the Soviets as they consider their Middle Eastern policy. The success or failure of the Soviets in addressing the bitter ethnic and cultural disputes in this region will have profound implications for the stability of the Middle East and Southwest Asia. In addition to these indigenous concerns, strategic factors such as natural resources and the region's location on critical trade routes will influence the Soviet approach to the area.

The Middle East/Southwest Asia will remain a vital region for Western interests as well. Although much has been done to diversify Western energy consumption and improve the efficiency of oil use, imported oil continues to represent over 40 percent of US energy consumption and 45-70 percent of that of our allies. Western economic infrastructures will remain closely tied to oil well into the next century, even if there were to be major technological breakthroughs in alternative fuel technologies.

These concerns will ensure continued US and Soviet interest in the region. Other factors, however, such as Iraqi regional hegemonic ambitions, potentially explosive indigenous issues, unstable and unpredictable governments, and expanding regional military capabilities, will strain the ability of either superpower to plan for or control the outcome of any potential conflict.

The Far East

The Soviets continue to reduce military forces in the Far East Theater of Operations (FETVD). However,

The nuclear-powered aircraft carrier USS Theodore Roosevelt (CVN-71) carries an air wing of 89-90 aircraft including fighter squadrons, light attack squadrons, medium attack squadrons, antisubmarine-warfare and electronic-warfare aircraft, early-warning aircraft, and ASW helicopters.

the Soviets have not been clear about what forces will be drawn down in Asia. The announced withdrawal of three-quarters of their forces from Mongolia has been completed and it appears that future Soviet reductions in the area will occur principally along the Soviet border with China in the Far East and Transbaykal MDs. Less emphasis is currently being placed on air and ground reductions in the Far East MD opposite Japan.

Soviet ground forces in the FETVD are expected to be reduced from the current 45 divisions to 38 by the mid-1990s. There will be an estimated 30-percent decrease in the overall number of tanks, but modern T-80, T-72, and improved T-72 tanks are expected to replace many older models. Along with the division reductions, there may be a conversion of perhaps 10 motorized rifle divisions (MRDs) to defensive machine-gun artillery divisions. Although little is known about the structure of the machine-gun artillery division, it is expected to be smaller than a MRD, with less mobility,

but with much of its original firepower retained. There, however, is currently no evidence that the four ground divisions opposite Japan in the FETVD, in the Northern Territories, on Sakhalin Island, or on the Kamchatka Peninsula will be included in the cuts.

Restructuring of Soviet air forces under way in the Far East is expected to continue through the 1990s and will result in unilateral reductions in the numbers of Soviet aircraft deployed to the region. There has already been a net reduction of three air regiments, and a total of 11 will reportedly be eliminated from the FETVD. If the 11 regiments are disbanded or withdrawn from the operational inventory, they would amount to a 40 percent drawdown of the total of 27 tactical air regiments active in the Far East MDs. It is likely that aircraft drawdowns will occur primarily, if not exclusively, in tactical air combat regiments. This would constrain an already limited Soviet capacity to conduct offensive operations against China without substantial augmentation. But combat capability will not decline as sharply as numbers, since the most advanced aircraft will be retained. Modernization of tactical air forces is continuing with the addition of the modern Su-24 Fencer E, MiG-29 Fulcrum, and Su-27 Flanker in the FETVD. The capability to employ Flanker in the long-range escort role is a recent combat enhancement in the FETVD and marks a new threat dimension for the US and Japan.

Bomber and strategic interceptor units remain unaffected by the restructuring. Intermediate- and long-range bomber forces retain the capability to attack China, Japan, the Pacific, and the continental US (CONUS).

The Soviets are also substantially upgrading their Far East air defense capabilities with the rapid buildup of SA-10 Grumble surface-to-air missile sites. The US estimates that a total of 27 SA-10 battalions will be deployed to the Far East. The total number of surface-to-air missiles in the FETVD will increase by about 25 percent by 1997 with much of the increase represented by the SA-10 and other modern air defense systems.

In the 1990s, the SOVPACFLT surface warship force level is expected to remain relatively constant, but combat potential will increase. This is due to an estimated 100 percent increase in the surface-to-surface missile capacity, 50-percent increase in surface-to-air missiles on surface warships, and a 40-percent increase in the number of ships with long-range ASW weapons. The projected growth of naval amphibious lift will be sufficient by the year 2000 to lift about 80 percent of the Soviet Pacific fleet SNI divisions' tactical assault forces — up from 50 percent today. SOVPACFLT's attack submarine force is expected to decline from about 70 combat submarines today to 60-65 units, but more will be modern, quiet boats with improved combat systems and greater numbers of weapons. For example, today's nuclear-powered cruise-missile attack submarine (SSGN) force of 18 active units carries 144 missiles; by the late 1990s, an estimated eight SSGNs will carry nearly 192 missiles. This means there will be fewer, more modern boats, with more missiles per boat.

US presence in the Far East is centered principally in Japan, South Korea, and the Philippines and is maintained through a series of bilateral and multilateral security arrangements. The Seventh Fleet is homeported in Japan, and the Air Force maintains tactical fighter wings at Yokota and Kadena Air Bases. US forces in Korea are part of a combined South Korean-American command that include a US Army division and two US Air Force tactical fighter wings. The Philippines hosts the principal maintenance, support, and storage base for units of the 180-ship Pacific Fleet, a base for antisubmarine operations, and an Air Force base with one tactical fighter wing. The total number of troops in the entire region is approximately 135,000.

The US envisions up to a 10-12 percent force reduction in the Pacific region by the mid-1990s. These reductions, coupled with pressure on overseas basing facilities, will likely place increasing limits on US forces in the region. Furthermore, raw numerical comparisons will continue to favor the Soviets, even after reductions by both superpowers. These numbers, however, must be tested against such factors as individual unit capabilities, technological differences, state of training, tactical innovativeness, the geography, allies, and unique defense requirements. These factors tend to favor the United States.

Most regional states perceive a continuing US presence in the region to be necessary for sustaining economic and political development, and precluding the rise of any regional hegemony. While the US will remain the major stabilizing influence, reduced superpower tensions will facilitate expanding interaction by the regional states. Thus, the regional balance increasingly will be dependent upon the capabilities of states within the region.

Implications for the Far East

In addition to traditional geopolitical issues, a number of factors will influence the balance of US and Soviet military strength and political influence in the region in the coming years. US bases in the region have drawn increasing criticism by indigenous personnel, and in the Philippines their future is now being negotiated. The near-term stability of the region will be affected by the slow but steady pace of Sino-Soviet rapprochement and a change in leadership in North Korea. The increasing capability of China and other states raises the potential for conflict in areas such as in the South China Sea over claims to the Spratly Islands. Any of these factors could alter the balance and possibly endanger otherwise favorable trends.

CONCLUSION

Prior to the advent of "new thinking," Soviet military policies sought to build and maintain forces capable of defeating the combined forces of all potential adversaries. As a matter of its declared policy, the Soviets now set less ambitious goals. Nevertheless, as a matter of capability, the Soviets remain the leading military power in Eurasia. By making use of a lengthier mobilization period, or if they could expect to exert force on a narrower front against a single country rather than against an alliance or global coalition, Soviet military forces could still make offensive use of that advantage.

As the nuclear arsenals of both superpowers are negotiated downward, the relative capabilities of conventional forces become more significant in attempts to maintain a balance. As the use of nuclear weapons becomes a more distant possibility, the potential for the employment of conventional forces may increase. Conflict avoidance will depend to a much greater extent on regional security arrangements and on a conventional capability that deters any inclination to resort to force to settle regional disputes.

VII

Prospects for the Future

A greater openness on the part of the Soviet Union and its military leadership has led to an increased willingness to engage in broader military-to-military exchanges with the United States. Here, the Slava-class guided missile cruiser Marshal Ustinov is seen arriving at Norfolk for a 1989 port call.

Today the free world may be facing one of its most difficult and serious challenges to date: how to respond to a rapidly changing environment in which the threats to which we have geared our security position for over 40 years have diminished, but where new instabilities and possible dangers pose new requirements. The challenge is difficult because the issues are so complex and paradoxical; it is serious because a miscalculated response could shape a world order that could thwart our aspirations for an increasingly peaceful and secure international environment. About the only certainty that now exists is the certainty of more change.

The role of the Soviet Union in an increasingly uncertain world is difficult to predict. For over four decades, the Soviet Union and its allies and proxies have been the principal threat to world peace and security. Moscow has used its power for intimidation, aggression, attempted dominance, and expansion. Real and lasting change in the Soviet threat can come only from a fundamental shift away from Moscow's historic reliance on force and the threat of force as instruments of foreign policy. In President Gorbachev's words, it means a "revolutionary transformation" of the Soviet state.

Encouraging events have occurred over the past year that indicate the Soviet Union may be heading toward such a revolutionary transformation, but the process is in its infancy and the ultimate outcome is not yet clear. The Soviet Union faces enormous obstacles to its transformation into a permanently less-threatening country. Decades of well-founded suspicion have left their legacy among the Soviet people as well as in the world community.

Soviet Military Power 1990 describes the many areas in which there have been changes in Soviet policy, doctrine, and relations with the rest of the world. But it is not yet clear to what extent these changes constitute enduring reform. The fundamental question is whether the Soviet Union will establish a government that is truly accountable to its citizens and to the rule of law — toward freedom, pluralistic democracy, and universal observance of human rights.

Although it is not possible to predict the future shape and direction of Soviet policy, there are changes that clearly can be identified, some with positive benefits and some with unknown consequences:

- Force reductions and withdrawals, along with the increasing disintegration of the Warsaw Pact, have greatly reduced the Soviets' capability to launch a multinational, unreinforced conventional attack into Western Europe.
- Soviet cooperation with the US in negotiating significant agreements holds great potential for reduction of the strategic, conventional, and chemical threat.
- The rise of nationalist sentiments within the Soviet Union, leading some republics to seek independence, calls into question the future cohesion of the USSR itself.

- The radical transformations required to cope with a failed economic and political system are fragmenting the Communist Party.
- The Soviets have displayed a more constructive approach in areas of their foreign policy, as evidenced by the withdrawal of Soviet troops from Afghanistan and reduction of support provided numerous radical regimes in Third World countries.

Despite these positive indications of change, there are troubling aspects that remain:

- The Soviets continue to modernize their strategic nuclear arsenal, resulting in a force that is generally more capable. The Soviets remain the only power on earth capable of destroying the US and its allies.
- As a result of basic facts of geography and demography, coupled with still-massive military expenditures, the Soviet Union will have the greatest military potential of any single country on the Eurasian landmass, likely retaining an army of around three million men, and weapons with thousands of nuclear warheads.
- The Soviets continue to provide roughly $15 billion in support of the threatening activities of some of their clients, such as Cuba, Afghanistan, Vietnam, Cambodia, and Ethiopia.

The implications of these realities are indeed significant. We are witnessing a transition from the bipolar confrontation that has characterized post-war international relations. Although warning time of a conventional Soviet attack on Western Europe has increased substantially, the magnitude of remaining Soviet military capabilities poses a profound challenge to our future planning. Military threats remain from a variety of sources.

Soviet military power must be assessed in light of these realities. The democratization of Eastern Europe and the increasing disintegration of the Warsaw Pact are positive developments, but it is not clear what the continuing modernization of the Soviet strategic nuclear arsenal and the internal turmoil within the Soviet Union mean for Western security. The immediate threat of a Soviet/Warsaw Pact multipronged armored thrust that pushes NATO into the Atlantic is nearly gone. What

VALDEZ/WHITE HOUSE

At the June 1990 Summit, President Bush made clear that as the USSR moves toward democracy and openness, US policy envisions going "beyond containment" and looks forward to welcoming the Soviet Union into the broader "commonwealth of nations."

remains is a Soviet Union with modern, increasingly capable conventional and nuclear weapons and a chemical/biological warfare capability. These weapons are controlled by a government that is being increasingly challenged at home and which cannot count on any support for offensive operations from its erstwhile allies. Responding to the threat is now complicated by the uncertain course of events in the Soviet Union. The West's response must be shaped by a vision that is anchored in the lessons of history. This will require modern, flexible, and secure forces that have the capability to respond to the unexpected.

The new environment presents the United States and the West with both opportunity and risk. We have the opportunity to help secure the positive trends toward freedom and cooperation and deflect or redirect the negative trends into more benign outcomes. Yet risk remains in the massive military capability, both conven-

tional and nuclear, that is controlled by a Soviet state that is beset with profound problems.

Our own security policy must take account of this uncertainty. Unilateral Western disarmament, which would remove our flexibility to deal with troublesome scenarios under the tenuous new conditions of international security, would weaken global deterrence and heighten global instability.

This is an extraordinary moment in history. Choices made by the United States and the Soviet Union will affect the direction of world affairs. Decisions made now will determine prospects for security and the advancement of freedom for generations to come. The United States must continue to encourage positive change, while maintaining the capability and flexibility to cope with — and deter — a still vast Soviet military capability at a moment of turmoil and uncertainty.

INDEX

INDEX

A

E

F

G

M

N

S